WILLIAMS-SONOMA

Rustic Italian

Simple, authentic recipes for everyday cooking

DOMENICA MARCHETTI

photography
MAREN CARUSO

weldon**owen**

contents

When I cook, my favorite everyday dishes to make for family and friends are uncomplicated ones—recipes that honor both ingredients and the seasons, with a nod to my heritage.

This book reflects my twin passions for eating Italian and eating locally. It is a collection of favorite recipes that I cook throughout the year, recipes that are both simple and beautiful in their simplicity. Each dish clearly evokes Italy, yet becomes something altogether new in my home kitchen.

I grew up in an Italian family in which food played a starring role. My mother was born and raised in Abruzzo, in central Italy, a region blessed with both mountains and coastline that takes pride in its rustic home cooking: hand-shaped pastas, simple roasted and grilled meats, pristine seafood prepared with few embellishments, and locally grown fruits and vegetables.

When my mother came to the United States in the 1950s, she brought her cooking traditions with her. But like any great home cook, she took those traditions and played around with them, working with ingredients available to her and experimenting with new riffs on classics. To this day, she remains a curious and innovative cook. I am proud to say I followed in my mother's footsteps.

As a girl, I spent my summers in Italy, and I return as often as I can for culinary inspiration. But I find my everyday inspiration right here at home. Farmers' markets offer an ever-growing variety of vegetables and fruits. The one near my house has two vendors who sell local, humanely raised meat. Farmstead cheeses—imported and domestic—are everywhere. And come summer, the tomatoes now rival the perfect, flavorful varieties I recall from Italy. It is a wonderful time to be someone who loves to cook. I hope you will make these recipes your own and share them with loved ones.

Buon appetito!

Domenica

antipasti

Ripe summer melon and buttery prosciutto has to be one of the greatest culinary marriages of all time. Here, I've lightly pickled the melon in a sweet-and-sour syrup to give this classic combination a fresh twist.

pickled melon with prosciutto, basil & mint

1 cantaloupe, 2½–3 lb (1.25–1.5 kg)

¼ cup (2 oz/60 g) sugar

¼ cup (2 fl oz/60 ml) white wine vinegar

Fine sea salt and freshly ground black pepper

8 thin slices prosciutto di Parma

1 tablespoon finely shredded fresh basil

1 tablespoon finely shredded fresh mint

serves 4

Set a colander over a bowl. Cut the cantaloupe in half and scoop out the seeds. Using a melon baller, scoop out the flesh, letting the fruit and any juices fall into the colander.

Measure the liquid that collected in the bowl. You should have about ¼ cup (2 fl oz/60 ml); if not, add enough water to equal ¼ cup. If you have more, discard the rest or reserve for another use. Pour the melon juice into a heavy-bottomed saucepan and add the sugar, vinegar, and ¼ teaspoon salt. Place over medium heat and cook, stirring once or twice, until the sugar is dissolved and the syrup comes to a boil. Boil until slightly thickened, about 2 minutes, then let cool for 10 minutes.

Put the melon balls in a bowl and pour in the syrup. Cover with plastic wrap and refrigerate until completely chilled, at least 2 hours or up to 4 hours.

To serve, arrange the prosciutto slices in ruffles on a serving platter. Using a slotted spoon, remove the melon balls from the syrup and arrange in clusters over the prosciutto. Scatter the basil and mint on top, season with a few grindings of pepper, and serve.

WINE SUGGESTION: SPARKLING WINE, SUCH AS PROSECCO DI CONEGLIANO OR PROSECCO DI VALDOBBIADENE

Burrata, a delicate ball of fresh mozzarella filled with curds and cream, is a remarkable experience all on its own. But I like to serve the cheese as part of an antipasti platter, with crostini, roasted peppers, and slices of grilled coppa. This dish is equally as tasty with *mozzarella di bufala*, which has more tang.

burrata with peppers & coppa

1 cup (8 oz/250 g) bottled roasted red or yellow peppers, drained and sliced

2 tablespoons extra-virgin olive oil, plus more for drizzling

1 tablespoon aged balsamic vinegar

1 tablespoon minced fresh flat-leaf parsley

Fine sea salt

12 thin slices hot or sweet coppa

1 large ball (8 oz/250 g) *burrata* cheese

Crostini (page 208) for serving

serves 4

In a bowl, combine the roasted peppers, olive oil, vinegar, parsley, and ¼ teaspoon salt and mix gently. Set aside.

In a large, dry grill pan or frying pan over high heat, cook 6 slices of the coppa until browned on the bottom and the edges begin to curl, 1–2 minutes. Turn and cook until browned and curling on the second side, 1–2 minutes longer. Transfer to a plate. Repeat to cook the remaining coppa.

Place the *burrata* in the center of a serving platter. Spoon the roasted pepper mixture around the cheese and arrange the coppa and crostini around the edges of the platter. Drizzle the cheese with additional olive oil, if desired, and serve.

WINE SUGGESTION: A FULL-BODIED WHITE FROM FRIULI, SUCH AS THOSE FROM THE DISTRICTS COLLIO OR COLLI ORIENTALI DEL FRIULI

Served as an antipasto in Umbria, Tuscany, and elsewhere in Italy, crostini are traditionally topped with such savory delights as sautéed chicken livers, porcini, or black truffles. Here's one of my favorite combinations—bitter Italian greens and flavorful cheese.

crostini with spicy broccoli rabe & pecorino

3 cloves garlic, minced

¼ cup (2 fl oz/60 ml) extra-virgin olive oil

1 small fresh hot chile, minced, or a generous pinch of red pepper flakes

1 lb (500 g) rapini (broccoli rabe), tough stems removed, leaves and tender stems chopped

Fine sea salt

20 Crostini (page 208)

½ cup (2 oz/60 g) shaved pecorino cheese

serves 6

In a large frying pan over medium-low heat, warm the garlic in the olive oil, stirring often, until softened but not browned, about 7 minutes. Sprinkle in the chile and stir to coat it with the oil. Add the broccoli rabe by the handful and, using tongs or a wooden spoon, toss and stir to coat with the oil after each addition.

Cover and cook until the greens are wilted, about 1 minute. Uncover, toss once more, re-cover, and cook at a gentle simmer until the greens are tender, 20–30 minutes. Stir in ¾ teaspoon salt. Raise the heat to medium and cook, uncovered, until most of the liquid has evaporated, about 10 minutes longer. Remove from the heat and let cool for 10 minutes, then transfer to a cutting board and chop finely.

Spoon the filling on top of the crostini and top with the pecorino shavings. Arrange the crostini on a platter and serve.

WINE SUGGESTION: PECORINO, A SOFT AND FRUITY WHITE FROM ABRUZZO OR LE MARCHE

I have a small fig tree in my backyard that produces a lovely little crop of plump, sweet Mission figs. They are delicious with prosciutto and tangy, buttery La Tur—a creamy cheese from Piedmont—in these sweet-and-savory summer crostini.

prosciutto, la tur & fig crostini

12 thin slices prosciutto di Parma, cut in half crosswise

24 Crostini (page 208)

8 oz (250 g) La Tur, Crescenza, or good-quality triple-crème Brie cheese

6 large or 12 small Mission figs, quartered if large, halved if small

Freshly ground black pepper

serves 8

Fold 1 piece of the prosciutto on top of each crostini. Spread or mound about 2 teaspoons of the cheese on the prosciutto and top with a wedge of fig. Arrange on a platter, grind a little pepper over the crostini, and serve.

WINE SUGGESTION: GAVI DI GAVI, THE FAMOUS CRISP WHITE FROM PIEDMONT

With its curvaceous bulb and feathery tops, fennel is beautiful to behold. It's also accommodating, at home in a raw crunchy salad or cooked until sweet, as in this elegant shrimp topping for crostini.

shrimp & fennel crostini

4 tablespoons (2 fl oz/60 ml) extra-virgin olive oil

2 fennel bulbs, quartered, cored, and cut crosswise into very thin slices (about 4 cups/12 oz/375 g), plus 1 tablespoon finely chopped fennel fronds

1 fresh bay leaf, or 2 dried bay leaves

1 small fresh hot chile, minced, or a generous pinch of red pepper flakes

Fine sea salt

4 teaspoons aged balsamic vinegar

12 medium shrimp, peeled and deveined

12 Crostini (page 208)

serves 4

In a large frying pan, heat 2 tablespoons of the olive oil over medium heat. Add the fennel bulbs, bay leaf, chile, and ½ teaspoon salt and stir well. Reduce the heat to medium-low and cook, stirring occasionally, until the fennel is soft and golden, about 20 minutes. Raise the heat to medium-high, drizzle in 2 teaspoons of the vinegar, and cook, stirring, for 2 minutes. Transfer to a bowl and cover to keep warm.

In the same frying pan, heat the remaining 2 tablespoons olive oil over medium heat. Arrange the shrimp in the pan in a single layer and sear on the first side, about 2 minutes. Turn and sear on the second side until opaque throughout, 2 minutes longer. Sprinkle with ½ teaspoon salt, drizzle with the remaining 2 teaspoons vinegar, and toss to coat. Remove from the heat.

Spoon about 1 tablespoon of the fennel mixture onto each crostini and top with a shrimp. Arrange on a platter, sprinkle with the chopped fennel fronds, and serve.

WINE SUGGESTION: A RICH WHITE FROM CAMPANIA, SUCH AS FALANGHINA OR FIANO DI AVELLINO

When my sister and I were little, our Italian aunts would often make us a snack of thick bread slices rubbed with tomato and seasoned with olive oil and salt. That classic combination is enhanced with creamy fresh ricotta and roasted cherry tomatoes.

bruschetta with caramelized tomatoes & ricotta

¼ cup (2 fl oz/60 ml) extra-virgin olive oil

2 cloves garlic, minced

1 tablespoon fennel seeds, coarsely pounded or crushed

Freshly ground black pepper and fine sea salt

1½ lb (750 g) cherry tomatoes, halved

FOR THE BRUSCHETTA

12 slices crusty country bread, cut into slices ½ inch (12 mm) thick

Extra-virgin olive oil for brushing

8 oz (250 g) fresh sheep's milk ricotta or well-drained cow's milk ricotta

serves 6

In a small bowl, stir together the olive oil, garlic, fennel seeds, and a generous grinding of pepper. Set aside and let stand for about 30 minutes.

Preheat the oven to 300°F (150°C). Arrange the tomatoes, cut side up, on a rimmed baking sheet. Spoon the olive oil mixture over the tomatoes and sprinkle with ½ teaspoon salt. Bake until the tomatoes are partially shriveled and browned in spots but still juicy, about 1½ hours. Transfer to a bowl, taking care to scrape any juices and browned bits from the baking sheet into the bowl.

To make the bruschetta, position a broiler pan 4 inches (10 cm) below the heat source and preheat the broiler. Arrange the bread slices on a large baking sheet and brush the tops with olive oil. Slip under the broiler and broil until the edges are lightly browned and the tops are golden, 1–2 minutes.

Spread a heaping tablespoon of the ricotta on each slice of bruschetta and top each with 1 heaping tablespoon of the caramelized tomatoes. Arrange the bruschetta on a platter and serve.

WINE SUGGESTION: A LOW-TANNIN RED, SUCH AS BARBERA D'ALBA OR BARBERA D'ASTI

These two-bite treasures are among my favorite antipasti.
Enjoy them plain, or drizzle with the sweet-tart balsamic syrup.

fried sage leaves with balsamic drizzle

½ cup (4 fl oz/125 ml)
balsamic vinegar

1 tablespoon honey or sugar

1 cup (5 oz/155 g)
unbleached all-purpose flour

Fine sea salt

1 cup (8 fl oz/250 ml)
sparkling water

1 large egg

Vegetable oil for frying

24 large, unblemished sage
leaves, with a bit of stem
still attached

serves 6–8

In a small saucepan, whisk together the vinegar and honey and bring to a boil over medium heat. Reduce the heat to medium-low and simmer until reduced to ¼ cup (2 fl oz/60 ml), about 10 minutes. Remove from the heat and cover to keep warm.

In a bowl, whisk together the flour and ½ teaspoon salt. Slowly pour in the water, whisking to prevent lumps. Add the egg and whisk until combined.

Pour oil into a frying pan to a depth of ½ inch (12 mm) and warm over medium-high heat until it registers 375°F (190°C) on a deep-frying thermometer, or until a small amount of batter sizzles and floats to the surface when dropped into the oil.

Holding a sage leaf by the stem, dip it into the batter and let any excess batter drip back into the bowl. Lower into the hot oil. Dip a few more leaves and add them to the pan, taking care not to overcrowd it. Fry the sage leaves until lightly browned, about 2 minutes. Using tongs or a fork, turn them and fry until golden, about 2 minutes longer. Using a skimmer or slotted spoon, transfer to paper towels to drain. Repeat to fry the remaining sage leaves.

Arrange the sage leaves on a platter and sprinkle with salt. Drizzle the balsamic syrup over the leaves (you may not need it all) and serve.

WINE SUGGESTION: PROSECCO, THE SPARKLING WHITE FROM THE VENETO

I could eat stuffed eggs every day. There are countless delicious ways to fill them, and here are two of my favorites, both starring classic Italian ingredients and salty flavors.

italian-style stuffed eggs

6 large eggs, hard-boiled and peeled

2 tablespoons unsalted butter, at room temperature

6 minced imported Italian or Spanish anchovy fillets, plus 1 whole anchovy

1 tablespoon small capers, rinsed, dried, and chopped, plus whole capers

1 tablespoon minced fresh flat-leaf parsley, plus 4 small whole leaves

Flaky sea salt and freshly ground black pepper

serves 4–6

STUFFED EGGS WITH ANCHOVIES, CAPERS & PARSLEY

Cut the eggs in half lengthwise. Gently pop out the yolks and press them through a fine-mesh sieve into a bowl. Set the whites aside.

Add the butter, minced anchovies, chopped capers, and minced parsley to the bowl and fold together until thoroughly combined. The mixture should be pasty and thick enough to roll. Divide it evenly and roll into 12 balls. Gently press the balls into the egg whites and arrange on a serving platter.

Cut the whole anchovy into 4 pieces and press them onto 4 of the stuffed eggs. Press some whole capers onto another 4 eggs, and garnish the last 4 eggs with the parsley leaves. If not serving right away, cover with plastic wrap and refrigerate for up to 2 hours. Let stand at room temperature for 30 minutes before serving. Season lightly with salt and pepper and serve.

6 large eggs, hard-boiled and peeled

⅓ cup (3 oz/90 g) imported Italian tuna in olive oil, drained and coarsely mashed

¼ cup (1¼ oz/40 g) coarsely chopped pitted black olives, such as Gaeta or Kalamata

2 tablespoons mayonnaise

Freshly ground black pepper

1 thin strip jarred roasted red pepper, cut into 12 small pieces

serves 4–6

STUFFED EGGS WITH TUNA & CHOPPED OLIVES

Cut the eggs in half lengthwise. Gently pop out the yolks and set 2 yolks aside. Press the remaining 4 yolks through a fine-mesh sieve into a bowl. Set the whites aside.

Add the tuna, olives, and mayonnaise to the bowl, season lightly with pepper, and fold together until thoroughly combined. The mixture should be pasty and thick enough to roll. Divide it evenly and roll into 12 balls. Gently press the balls into the egg whites and arrange on a serving platter.

Press a piece of roasted pepper onto each stuffed egg. Press the reserved egg yolks through a fine-mesh sieve on top of the stuffed eggs. If not serving right away, cover with plastic wrap and refrigerate for up to 2 hours. Let stand at room temperature for 30 minutes before serving. Season lightly with pepper and serve.

WINE SUGGESTION: A FULL-BODIED WHITE, SUCH AS VERMENTINO FROM SARDINIA OR PIGATO FROM LIGURIA

What can I say? I've always adored little bites of bacon-wrapped anything, from shrimp to figs, especially when they are plumped and crisped under the broiler. Rich, mild blue *Cambozola* cheese and prosciutto give new life to a classic.

cambozola-stuffed dates wrapped in prosciutto

24 Medjool dates, pitted

3 oz (90 g) *Cambozola* cheese

12 thin slices prosciutto di Parma, cut in half lengthwise

serves 8–12

Position a broiler pan 4 inches (10 cm) below the heat source and preheat the broiler.

Stuff each date with about ½ teaspoon of the cheese and wrap a strip of prosciutto around each one. Arrange on a rimmed baking sheet. Slip under the broiler and broil until the prosciutto is crispy and the cheese is bubbling, about 5 minutes.

Transfer the dates to a serving platter and serve hot.

WINE SUGGESTION: A LIGHT-BODIED RED, SUCH AS PINOT NERO FROM ALTO ADIGE

My mother made classic *giardiniera* pickle almost every year, with crunchy pieces of carrot, cauliflower, onion, and bell pepper. Here is my shortcut variation, topped with spicy bread crumbs.

pickled cauliflower with chile bread crumbs

⅓ cup (3 fl oz/80 ml) red wine vinegar

Fine sea salt

1 clove garlic, minced

1 head cauliflower, purple if available, cut into bite-size florets

3 tablespoons chopped fresh herbs, such as flat-leaf parsley, basil, or mint, or a mixture

2 tablespoons extra-virgin olive oil

1 small fresh hot chile, minced, or a generous pinch of red pepper flakes

1½ cups (3 oz/90 g) fresh bread crumbs

serves 6–8

In a small bowl, whisk together the vinegar, 2 tablespoons water, ½ teaspoon salt, and the garlic. Set aside.

Place a steamer basket in a large saucepan and fill the pan with water up to but not touching the bottom of the basket. Bring the water to a boil over high heat. Add the cauliflower to the basket, cover, and steam until just tender, about 5 minutes.

Transfer the cauliflower to a large bowl and sprinkle with the herbs. Pour the vinegar mixture over and toss to coat thoroughly. Let marinate for 30 minutes, stirring every 5 minutes so that the vinegar is evenly absorbed.

Meanwhile, in a frying pan, heat the olive oil over medium-high heat. Add the chile and cook until fragrant, about 1 minute. Add the bread crumbs and stir to coat with the oil. Sprinkle with ¼ teaspoon salt and sauté until the crumbs are crisped and golden brown, 5–7 minutes.

Transfer the cauliflower to a serving bowl, sprinkle with the bread crumbs, and serve.

WINE SUGGESTION: A WHITE WITH GOOD ACIDITY, SUCH AS VERNACCIA DI SAN GIMIGNANO

My husband is one of those people who can pop a whole wedge of lemon in his mouth and gobble it up like chocolate. I love lemons, but I just can't do it. Grilled lemons, however, are a different story—the hot, smoky heat caramelizes the flesh and softens the rinds.

grilled shrimp & lemon skewers

3 tablespoons
extra-virgin olive oil

2 tablespoons fresh
lemon juice

3 cloves garlic, minced

2 teaspoons minced fresh
rosemary

Generous pinch of red
pepper flakes

Fine sea salt

1 lb (16 oz/500 g) extra-
large shrimp (about 32)

16 wooden skewers, soaked
in water for 30 minutes

2 lemons, cut into
16 wedges

serves 8

In a large bowl, combine the olive oil, lemon juice, garlic, minced rosemary, red pepper flakes, and ½ teaspoon salt and whisk until well blended. Add the shrimp and toss gently to coat thoroughly with the marinade. Cover and let marinate at room temperature for about 30 minutes.

Prepare a fire in a charcoal grill or preheat a gas grill to medium-high.

Drain the skewers and thread each with 1 shrimp, 1 lemon wedge, and then 1 more shrimp.

Arrange the skewers on the grill grate and grill, turning once or twice, until the shrimp and lemons are nicely browned in places and the shrimp are opaque throughout, about 5 minutes total. Transfer the skewers to a serving platter and serve right away.

WINE SUGGESTION: A CRISP, MODERATELY ACIDIC AND FRUITY WHITE, SUCH AS VERDICCHIO DEI CASTELLI JESI

Rich and delicate, fresh sheep's milk ricotta is sweeter and firmer than the traditional cow's milk versions. It's a little harder to come by, so if you are unable to find it, use another good-quality fresh ricotta, but be sure to drain thoroughly.

baked ricotta with toasted pine nuts

12 oz (375 g) fresh sheep's milk ricotta

2 tablespoons extra-virgin olive oil

Fine sea salt and freshly ground black pepper

1–2 tablespoons pine nuts

2 large fresh basil leaves, finely shredded

Crostini (page 208) for serving

serves 4–6

Preheat the oven to 375°F (190°C). Put the ricotta in a small baking dish, drizzle with the olive oil, and sprinkle a little salt and pepper over the top. Bake until lightly browned, 15–20 minutes.

While the ricotta is baking, put the pine nuts in a small, dry frying pan and toast over medium heat, shaking the pan often to prevent burning, until lightly browned, 2–3 minutes. Immediately pour into a small bowl and let cool.

Transfer the ricotta to a serving plate and spoon the oil from the baking dish over it. Scatter the toasted pine nuts and basil ribbons on top. Arrange the crostini around the edges of the plate and serve right away.

WINE SUGGESTION: PECORINO, A SOFT WHITE FROM ABRUZZO OR LE MARCHE

The farmers' market that sets up every Wednesday outside my local library has only a dozen stalls, but in summer there is a cornucopia of plums, from green gage to Italian prune. A stint on the grill makes them a sweet partner for chicken.

grilled chicken & plum skewers

½ cup (4 fl oz/125 ml) extra-virgin olive oil

2 tablespoons aged balsamic vinegar

1 tablespoon minced fresh sage

Fine sea salt and freshly ground black pepper

8 boneless, skinless chicken thighs, each cut into 4 pieces

8 wooden skewers, soaked in water for 30 minutes

4 plums, pitted and quartered

1 large red onion, cut into 8 wedges

serves 8

In a bowl, whisk together the olive oil, vinegar, sage, 1 teaspoon salt, and a generous grinding of pepper.

Put the chicken in a large bowl or a zipper-lock plastic bag. Pour about three-fourths of the marinade over the chicken and seal or cover tightly. Reserve the rest of the marinade for basting. Let the chicken marinate at room temperature for 20 minutes or in the refrigerator for at least 30 minutes or up to 3 hours.

Prepare a fire in a charcoal grill or preheat a gas grill to medium-high. Drain the skewers and thread each with the chicken chunks, plum quarters, and onion wedges in the following order: chicken, plum, chicken, onion, chicken, plum, chicken.

Arrange the skewers on the grill grate and grill, turning them several times and basting with the reserved marinade, until the meat is charred in a few places and the juices run clear when poked with a fork, 8–10 minutes total. Transfer to a serving platter and serve right away.

WINE SUGGESTION: A FRUITY RED, SUCH AS DOLCETTO D'ALBA OR DOLCETTO DI DOGLIANI

Where I come from, you're only as good as your last batch of meatballs. They must be tender, yet firm enough to hold up in sauce. These shine in a simple sauce of tomato and chard.

meatballs in swiss chard & tomato sauce

FOR THE MEATBALLS

1 cup (2 oz/60 g) fresh bread crumbs

2 tablespoons milk

¾ lb (375 g) *each* ground pork and ground veal

2 tablespoons freshly grated Parmigiano-Reggiano cheese

1 clove garlic, minced

1 tablespoon minced fresh flat-leaf parsley

1 tablespoon dry white wine

Fine sea salt and freshly ground black pepper

1 large egg, lightly beaten

FOR THE SAUCE

2 cloves garlic, very thinly sliced

2 tablespoons extra-virgin olive oil

1 lb (500 g) Swiss chard, stems chopped, leaves shredded crosswise

Fine sea salt

Pinch of red pepper flakes

¼ cup (1½ oz/45 g) golden raisins

3 cups (24 fl oz/750 ml) tomato sauce, preferably homemade (page 209)

serves 8–12

To make the meatballs, preheat the oven to 400°F (200°C). In a small bowl, combine the bread crumbs and milk and let stand for 5 minutes. In a large bowl, combine the pork and veal, soaked bread crumbs, cheese, garlic, parsley, wine, ¼ teaspoon salt, and pepper to taste. Add the egg and mix thoroughly. Form into 24 small meatballs about the size of a golf ball and arrange on an ungreased rimmed baking sheet. Bake, turning the meatballs once, until browned on both sides, about 30 minutes.

To make the sauce, in a large frying pan over medium-low heat, warm the garlic in the olive oil, stirring often, until it begins to release its fragrance, about 3 minutes. Stir in the chard stems, raise the heat to medium, and cook until softened, about 5 minutes. Add the leaves, cover, and cook until wilted, about 5 minutes. Add ½ teaspoon salt and the red pepper flakes and cook, uncovered, until the chard is tender, about 15 minutes.

Stir in the raisins and ½ cup (4 fl oz/125 ml) water. Cover and cook until the raisins are softened, about 5 minutes. Add the tomato sauce and bring to a simmer. Reduce the heat to medium-low, add the meatballs, cover, and simmer gently so the meatballs absorb some of the sauce, about 10 minutes.

Scoop the meatballs into a serving bowl or individual small bowls, top with the sauce, and serve right away, with bread for sopping up the sauce, if you like.

WINE SUGGESTION: A LIGHT RED, SUCH AS MONTEPULCIANO D'ABRUZZO OR VALPOLICELLA

These golden rice croquettes with oozing cheese at their centers are sold in casual lunch spots called *rosticcerie* in many parts of Italy. If you like, assemble and fry the croquettes ahead of time, then freeze. Reheat in a 400°F (200°C) oven for 15 minutes.

fontina-stuffed saffron rice croquettes

1 tablespoon unsalted butter

1 tablespoon extra-virgin olive oil

½ yellow onion, finely diced

1 cup (7 oz/220 g) Arborio, Carnaroli, or other risotto rice

¼ cup (2 fl oz/60 ml) dry white wine

3–4 cups (24–32 fl oz/ 750 ml–1 l) chicken broth, preferably homemade (page 209), heated to a simmer

½ teaspoon saffron threads

1 tablespoon minced fresh flat-leaf parsley

Freshly ground black pepper

¾ cup (3 oz/90 g) freshly grated Parmigiano-Reggiano cheese

In a large, heavy-bottomed saucepan over medium heat, melt the butter with the olive oil. When the butter begins to sizzle, add the onion and sauté until soft and translucent, about 7 minutes.

Add the rice and stir to coat thoroughly with the fat. Raise the heat to medium-high, pour in the wine, and let it bubble until most of the liquid has evaporated, 1–2 minutes. Stir in a ladleful of the broth, reduce the heat to medium, and cook, stirring all the while, until the broth is absorbed. Add another ladleful of broth and cook until absorbed, still stirring often. Reduce the heat to medium-low if necessary to maintain a gentle simmer.

In a small bowl, dissolve the saffron threads in a spoonful of the hot broth and pour into the risotto, stirring to mix well. Continue to cook the risotto, adding broth a ladleful at a time and stirring until it is absorbed before adding more, until the rice is creamy and just tender, about 25 minutes. The grains should be the tiniest bit firm in the center when you bite into them.

Remove from the heat and stir in the parsley and a generous grinding of pepper. Fold in the Parmigiano. Scrape the risotto into a large baking dish and spread in an even layer. Cover and refrigerate until well chilled, about 1 hour.

1½ cups (7½ oz/235 g) unbleached all-purpose flour

3 large eggs, lightly beaten

2 cups (8 oz/250 g) dried bread crumbs

8 oz (250 g) fontina cheese, preferably Fontina Val d'Aosta, cut into ½-inch (12-mm) cubes

Vegetable oil for frying

serves 8–12

Place the flour, eggs, and bread crumbs in 3 separate shallow bowls or pie tins. Using your fingers, scoop a heaping tablespoon of the chilled risotto into the palm of your hand. Press a cube of fontina into the risotto and mold the rice into a ball or oval around the cheese.

Roll the croquette first in the flour, then the eggs, and finally the bread crumbs. Place on a rimmed baking sheet. Repeat to fill and shape the rest of the croquettes.

Pour oil into a large, deep frying pan or heavy-bottomed saucepan to a depth of 1 inch (2.5 cm) and heat over medium-high heat until it registers 350°F (180°C) on a deep-frying thermometer, or until a small pinch of bread crumbs sizzles immediately when dropped into the oil. Gently lower 6–8 croquettes into the hot oil, being careful not to crowd the pan, and fry, turning once or twice, until lightly browned on all sides, 3–4 minutes total. Using a slotted spoon, transfer the croquettes to a platter lined with paper towels to drain. Repeat to fry the remaining croquettes. Arrange in a deep platter and serve hot or warm.

WINE SUGGESTION: CERASUOLO, AN ITALIAN ROSÉ, OR A LIGHT-TO-MEDIUM RED, SUCH AS VALPOLICELLA OR BARDOLINO

Buy the freshest salmon you can find for this flavorful starter. Choose wild salmon, which has a better flavor and texture than farmed. This recipe is easily doubled to serve more.

salmon crudo with red onion & fried capers

½ lb (250 g) fresh sushi-grade skinless salmon, wrapped tightly in plastic wrap and frozen for 30 minutes

¼ cup (2 fl oz/60 ml) extra-virgin olive oil

1 tablespoon small capers, rinsed and dried

1 tablespoon fresh lemon juice

2 teaspoons minced fresh flat-leaf parsley

¼ red onion, very thinly sliced

Flaky sea salt and freshly ground black pepper

Lemon wedges for serving

serves 4

Using a sharp knife, slice the salmon against the grain into very thin slices. Arrange the slices on a serving platter, overlapping them slightly. Cover with plastic wrap and refrigerate for 30–60 minutes.

In a small frying pan, heat the olive oil over medium-high heat. Carefully add the capers (they will spatter). Fry, swirling the pan gently to move the capers around, until they are golden brown, 30–60 seconds. Transfer the capers to a paper towel–lined plate. Pour the oil into a small bowl and let cool for 5 minutes.

Add the lemon juice and parsley to the bowl with the oil and whisk until the dressing is emulsified.

Arrange the red onion on top of the salmon and drizzle with the dressing. Season lightly with salt and pepper. Scatter the capers on top and serve with lemon wedges.

WINE SUGGESTION: FRANCIACORTA BRUT, A RICH SPARKLING WINE, OR FIANO DI AVELLINO, A STILL WHITE FROM CAMPANIA

Although traditional caponata is sautéed, I like the smokiness that grilling imparts to summer squash and eggplant. Try the mixture as a topping for crostini or spooned on bruschetta.

grilled summer vegetables

2 cloves garlic, crushed flat but left whole

½ cup (4 fl oz/125 ml) extra-virgin olive oil

2 ribs celery, diced

1 cup (5 oz/155 g) coarsely chopped green olives

2 medium or 1 large eggplant, cut crosswise into slices ¾ inch (2 cm) thick

1 zucchini or other green summer squash, halved lengthwise

1 large red onion, cut crosswise into thick slices

Fine sea salt and freshly ground black pepper

3 wooden skewers, soaked in water for 30 minutes

12 cherry tomatoes

1 tablespoon capers, drained and coarsely chopped

1 tablespoon sugar

2 tablespoons red wine vinegar, plus more if needed

1 tablespoon balsamic vinegar

1 tablespoon minced fresh flat-leaf parsley

1 teaspoon minced fresh mint

serves 6–8

Prepare a fire in a charcoal grill or preheat a gas grill to medium-high.

In a large frying pan over medium heat, warm the garlic in ¼ cup (2 fl oz/ 60 ml) of the olive oil until the garlic is sizzling, about 2 minutes. Stir in the celery and sauté until beginning to soften, about 3 minutes. Stir in the olives and cook for 1 minute. Remove from the heat.

Brush the eggplant, zucchini, and onion with the remaining ¼ cup (2 fl oz/60 ml) oil and season with salt and pepper. Drain the skewers and thread 4 tomatoes on each. Arrange the eggplant, zucchini, and onion slices on the grill grate and grill until nicely charred but still somewhat firm, about 3 minutes per side. Add the tomatoes and grill until charred in spots, 1–2 minutes. Collect the vegetables in a bowl as they finish. When the vegetables are cool enough to handle, cut the eggplant, zucchini, and onion slices into bite-size pieces, and cut the tomatoes in half or leave whole.

Return the frying pan to medium heat and add the grilled vegetables and the capers. Cook just until heated through, about 2 minutes. Stir in the sugar and the vinegars, raise the heat to high, and cook for 1 minute. Remove from the heat and stir in the minced parsley and mint. Taste and adjust the seasoning, adding a splash of red wine vinegar if it needs brightening. Let stand for 30 minutes to allow the flavors to blend. Spoon into a small bowl and serve.

WINE SUGGESTION: ANY NUMBER OF REDS FROM SOUTHERN ITALY, SUCH AS NERO D'AVOLA FROM SICILY OR SALICE SALENTINO FROM PUGLIA

I hate to think that I used to throw out the leafy tops of beets, which are packed with earthy flavor. Now I put them in soups, sauces, and egg dishes, like this savory tart.

beet green & parmesan tart

4 cloves garlic, thinly sliced

5 tablespoons (3 fl oz/80 ml) extra-virgin olive oil

1 lb (500 g) beet greens, tough stems removed, leaves and tender stems coarsely chopped

5 large eggs

2 tablespoons unbleached all-purpose flour

1 cup (4 oz/125 g) freshly grated Parmigiano-Reggiano cheese

Fine sea salt and freshly ground black pepper

serves 8–12

In a large sauté pan over medium-low heat, warm the garlic in 3 tablespoons of the olive oil, stirring often, until softened, about 7 minutes. Add half of the beet greens and toss to coat the greens with the oil. Raise the heat to medium, cover, and cook until wilted, about 1 minute. Add the rest of the greens to the pan, again turning with tongs to coat with the oil. Cover again and cook, tossing occasionally, until all of the greens are wilted and tender, about 15 minutes. Remove from the heat and let cool.

Position a broiler pan 4 inches (10 cm) below the heat source and preheat the broiler.

In a bowl, whisk together the eggs, flour, cheese, ½ teaspoon salt, and pepper to taste. Gently fold in the cooled greens.

In a well-seasoned 12-inch (30-cm) cast-iron or other heavy-bottomed ovenproof nonstick frying pan, heat the remaining 2 tablespoons olive oil over medium heat. Pour in the egg mixture and reduce the heat to medium-low. Cook the tart until lightly browned on the bottom and the middle is almost set, about 7 minutes. (Use a small spatula to lift the tart after 5 minutes to see if the bottom is browned.)

Slip under the broiler and broil until the top is lightly browned and the tart is sizzling hot, 2–3 minutes. Remove from the oven and let cool for 5 minutes. Use a spatula or knife to loosen the tart from the pan and slide it onto a serving platter. Cut into thin wedges and serve warm or at room temperature.

WINE SUGGESTION: A REFRESHING LEMONY WHITE, SUCH AS SOAVE OR SOAVE CLASSICO

Torte salate, or savory tarts, are enjoyed as an antipasto or sometimes as a quick lunch in Italy. They feature all kinds of vegetables—literally from artichokes to zucchini—but tomato tarts are probably my favorite, especially when punched up with pungent blue cheese.

slow-roasted tomato & gorgonzola tarts

FOR THE ROASTED TOMATOES

8 medium round tomatoes, about 1 lb (500 g) total weight, halved lengthwise

3 tablespoons extra-virgin olive oil

Fine sea salt and freshly ground black pepper

FOR THE PASTRY DOUGH

1 cup (5 oz/155 g) unbleached all-purpose flour, plus more for dusting

Fine sea salt

½ cup (4 oz/125 g) fresh ricotta cheese or small-curd cottage cheese

½ cup (4 oz/125 g) cold unsalted butter, cut into ½-inch (12-mm) dice

1 tablespoon Dijon mustard

3 oz (90 g) Gorgonzola or other blue cheese, crumbled

1 large egg whisked with ½ cup (4 fl oz/125 ml) heavy cream

Freshly ground black pepper

Arugula for garnish

serves 8

To make the tomatoes, preheat the oven to 300°F (150°C). Place the tomato halves, cut side up, on a rimmed baking sheet. Drizzle the olive oil over them and season lightly with salt and pepper. Roast until the tomatoes are partially collapsed and wrinkled but still juicy, about 3 hours. Set aside.

Meanwhile, make the dough: In a food processor, combine the flour and ½ teaspoon salt and pulse to mix. Scatter the cheese and butter around the bowl and pulse until the mixture begins to come together. Turn the dough out onto a lightly floured work surface and pat it into a disk. Wrap in plastic wrap and refrigerate for at least 1 hour or up to overnight.

Divide the dough into 4 equal pieces. On a lightly floured work surface, roll each piece out into a 6-inch (15-cm) circle. Press the circles into four 4½-inch (11.5-cm) fluted tart pans with removable sides. Fold the overhang in, pressing it against the inside rim. Place the pans on a baking sheet and refrigerate for 30 minutes.

Increase the oven temperature to 425°F (220°C). Line the tart shells with parchment paper or aluminum foil and fill with pie weights or dried beans. Bake for 8 minutes. Remove the parchment and pie weights and bake until the shells are set and only just beginning to turn pale gold, about 2 minutes longer. Remove from the oven but leave the tart shells on the baking sheet. Reduce the oven temperature to 350°F (180°C).

If the bottoms of the shells have puffed up, poke them in a few places with a cake tester. Brush the bottoms of the shells with a thin coating of mustard. Arrange 3–4 tomato halves in each shell and sprinkle the cheese over them. Pour the egg-cream mixture into the shells (do not overfill). Season lightly with pepper. Bake until the tarts are puffed and golden brown, about 25 minutes. Transfer to a wire rack and let cool for 20 minutes. Remove the sides from the pans and gently turn them over to remove the metal bottoms. Arrange the tarts on a serving platter, sprinkle with arugula, and serve warm.

WINE SUGGESTION: SCHIAVA, A MEDIUM-TO-LIGHT RED FROM ALTO ADIGE

soups & salads

On a trip to Livorno years ago, I made two important discoveries. First, that it is the birthplace of one of my favorite painters, Amadeo Modigliani. Second, this fish stew, which has become a favorite dish in my cooking repertoire.

livorno fish stew

2 dozen small clams, such as Manila or littleneck, scrubbed

3 tablespoons extra-virgin olive oil, plus more for drizzling

1 yellow onion, finely chopped

4 tablespoons (1/3 oz/10 g) minced fresh parsley

Pinch of red pepper flakes

1/2 lb (250 g) cleaned baby octopus or calamari, cut into large pieces

2 tablespoons red wine vinegar

1 bay leaf

1 cup (8 fl oz/250 ml) full-bodied red wine

1 can (28 oz/875 g) diced tomatoes

1 1/2 lb (750 g) white fish, such as rockfish or red snapper, cut into large pieces

8 shell-on jumbo shrimp, with heads attached

Bruschetta (page 20)

serves 6–8

Put the clams in a large, dry frying pan over medium-high heat. Cover and cook, shaking the pan occasionally, until all the clams have opened, about 5 minutes. Using tongs, transfer to a bowl and cover to keep warm. Strain the pan juices into a clean bowl through a fine-mesh sieve lined with a damp paper towel. Set aside.

In a soup pot, combine the olive oil, onion, 2 tablespoons of the parsley, and the red pepper flakes. Sauté over medium-low heat until the onion is softened, 7–8 minutes. Add the octopus, vinegar, and bay leaf and stir. Raise the heat to medium-high and simmer for 1 minute. Stir in the wine, reduce the heat to medium, and simmer until most of the wine has been absorbed, about 5 minutes. Stir in 3 cups (21 oz/655 g) of the tomatoes and return to a simmer. Reduce the heat to maintain a gentle simmer and cook until thickened, about 20 minutes.

Add the reserved clams and clam juice, the remaining 1 cup (7 oz/220 g) tomatoes, the fish, and the shrimp to the pot and stir gently to mix. Cook just until the shrimp have turned pink and the fish is opaque throughout, about 5 minutes. Remove from the heat and sprinkle in the remaining 2 tablespoons parsley. Discard the bay leaf. Divide the bruschetta among shallow bowls. Ladle the stew over the bread and serve.

WINE SUGGESTION: MORELLINO DI SCANSANO, A SANGIOVESE GROWN IN THE MAREMMA REGION, OR A DRY WHITE FROM THE SAME AREA, SUCH AS VERMENTINO BOLGHERI

Make this comforting soup in autumn, when you can find fresh celery with heads full of leafy tops at the farmers' market. Put some of those tops in the soup and use the rest to flavor broths, sauces, and stews, and to toss in fall salads. I enrich the soup with a touch of heavy cream; for a lighter version, omit the dairy.

cream of celery soup with pecorino crisps

2 tablespoons unsalted butter

2 tablespoons extra-virgin olive oil

1 small yellow onion, diced

1 carrot, peeled and cut into rounds

1 small russet potato, peeled and diced

1 bunch celery, including some of the tops and leaves, chopped, plus a handful of leaves for garnish

Fine sea salt and freshly ground black pepper

2 cups (16 fl oz/500 ml) vegetable or chicken broth, preferably homemade (page 209), plus more as needed

¼ cup (2 fl oz/60 ml) heavy cream (optional)

1 tablespoon minced fresh flat-leaf parsley

¼ cup (1 oz/30 g) shredded *pecorino romano* cheese

¼ cup (1 oz/30 g) finely grated *pecorino romano* cheese

serves 6–8

In a Dutch oven or soup pot, melt the butter with the olive oil over medium heat. Reduce the heat to medium-low and stir in the onion, carrot, and potato. Cook, stirring occasionally, until the onion is translucent and the carrot is bright orange, about 15 minutes.

Add the celery and ½ cup (4 fl oz/125 ml) water. Season with 1 teaspoon salt and a few grindings of pepper. Cover and cook without browning (reduce the heat to low if necessary) until the vegetables are tender, 40–50 minutes. Add 1 cup (8 fl oz/250 ml) of the broth, cover, and cook until all of the vegetables are soft, about 10 minutes longer. Poke a few of the larger pieces with a fork to test. Remove from the heat.

Using an immersion blender, purée the soup until smooth. Alternately, transfer to a stand blender, purée in batches, and return to the pot. Add more broth as needed when blending. Return the pot to medium-low heat and stir in the cream, if using. Bring to a simmer and add up to 1 more cup of broth to thin the soup to the desired consistency. Sprinkle in the parsley. Remove from the heat and cover to keep warm.

Preheat the oven to 350°F (180°C). Line a rimmed baking sheet with a Silpat mat or parchment paper. In a bowl, stir together the shredded and grated cheeses. Drop 8 small mounds, each about 2 tablespoons, on the prepared baking sheet, spreading them out a bit. Bake until the cheese has spread out and turned bubbly and golden brown, about 8 minutes. Using a spatula, transfer the crisps to a plate and let cool.

Ladle the soup into bowls. Float a crisp on top of each portion and garnish with celery leaves.

WINE SUGGESTION: ORVIETO SUPERIORE OR ORVIETO CLASSICO, A CRISP WHITE FROM THE AREA SURROUNDING THE TOWN OF ORVIETO, IN UMBRIA

Pasta in broth is the first solid food I ate, and I could eat it every day for the rest of my life without tiring of it. Homemade chicken broth makes the best soup, of course, and spinach enriches its flavor—and nutritional value—even more.

chicken soup with broken noodles & spinach

8 cups (64 fl oz/2 l) chicken broth, preferably homemade (page 209)

1⅓ cups (6 oz/185 g) capellini, *fedelini,* or other thin dried noodles, broken into 1-inch (2.5-cm) lengths

4 cups (4 oz/125 g) spinach, tough stems removed

1 cup (4 oz/125 g) freshly grated Parmigiano-Reggiano cheese

serves 4

In a soup pot over medium heat, bring the chicken broth to a boil. Reduce the heat to medium-low and slowly pour in the noodles (if you pour too quickly, the broth may boil over). Stir the noodles to prevent sticking, then stir in the spinach, a handful at a time. Cover partially and cook at a gentle simmer, stirring from time to time, until the noodles are just tender, 3–8 minutes (the cooking time will depend on the brand and size of the noodles).

Remove from the heat and stir in half of the cheese. Ladle the soup into bowls, garnish with some of the remaining cheese, and serve.

WINE SUGGESTION: A LIGHT-TO-MEDIUM RED, SUCH AS MONTEPULCIANO D'ABRUZZO OR VALPOLICELLA

This fall dish was inspired by long hours of perusing my mom's collection of Italian cooking magazines dating back to the early 1960s. Simple puréed soups featuring seasonal ingredients were as popular then as they are today—with good reason.

carrot & winter squash soup with pancetta

1½ lb (750 g) butternut squash, peeled and cut into chunks

1 lb (500 g) carrots, peeled and cut into chunks

2 yellow onions, cut into chunks

3 large cloves garlic, coarsely chopped

4 fresh thyme sprigs

2 tablespoons coarsely chopped fresh basil

1 tablespoon coarsely chopped fresh flat-leaf parsley

Fine sea salt and freshly ground pepper

¼ cup (2 fl oz/60 ml) extra-virgin olive oil, plus more for drizzling

4 cups (32 fl oz/1 l) chicken broth, preferably homemade (page 209), plus more for thinning the soup

6 oz (185 g) pancetta, cut into ¾-inch (2-cm) dice

serves 6–8

Preheat the oven to 425°F (220°C). In a roasting pan, combine the squash, carrots, onions, garlic, thyme, basil, and parsley. Season with 1 teaspoon salt and a grinding of pepper. Drizzle the olive oil over the vegetables and toss to coat. Roast, stirring every 15 minutes, until tender and browned in spots, about 45 minutes.

Remove the vegetables from the oven and discard the thyme sprigs. Transfer the vegetables to a soup pot and add 4 cups of the broth. Using an immersion blender, purée the soup until smooth. Alternately, transfer to a stand blender, purée the soup in 2 batches, and return to the pot.

Add more broth to thin the soup to the desired consistency. Place over medium-low heat and cook until warmed through, about 10 minutes.

Meanwhile, in a dry frying pan over medium-low heat, sauté the pancetta until crisped and some of the fat is rendered, 12–15 minutes. Transfer to paper towels to drain.

Ladle the soup into bowls, garnish with a few of the pancetta "croutons," drizzle with olive oil, and serve.

WINE SUGGESTION: A CRISP WHITE SUCH AS SOAVE CLASSICO

Wild rice is not a traditional Italian food, but its earthy flavor goes beautifully with the other classic Italian ingredients in this fall soup. I serve this as a first course at Thanksgiving to honor both my Italian and my American heritages.

wild rice soup with porcini & escarole

1 oz (30 g) dried porcini mushrooms, steeped in 1½ cups (12 fl oz/375 ml) boiling water for 30 minutes

1 tablespoon unsalted butter

2 tablespoons olive oil

2 small leeks, white and pale green parts only, thinly sliced

½ lb (8 oz/250 g) mixed fresh mushrooms, brushed clean and thinly sliced

Fine sea salt and freshly ground black pepper

½ cup (4 fl oz/125 ml) dry white wine

1 small head escarole, thinly sliced crosswise

1½ cups (10½ oz/330 g) wild rice blend (a mix of wild and brown rices)

6 cups (48 fl oz/1.5 l) chicken broth, preferably homemade (page 209)

½ cup (4 fl oz/125 ml) heavy cream

2 tablespoons minced fresh flat-leaf parsley

serves 4

Drain the porcini, reserving the liquid, then chop and set aside. Strain the mushroom broth into a clean bowl through a fine-mesh sieve lined with a damp paper towel.

In a soup pot over medium heat, melt the butter with the olive oil. Add the leeks and sauté until softened, about 7 minutes. Stir in the fresh mushrooms and the porcini and season with salt and pepper. Cover partially and cook, stirring occasionally, until the mushrooms are tender, about 10 minutes.

Raise the heat to high, stir in the wine, and simmer for 1 minute. Return the heat to medium and add the escarole, a handful at a time, stirring to mix well and adding more as the escarole in the pot begins to wilt. Pour in the reserved porcini broth, reduce the heat to medium-low, cover, and cook until all of the escarole is wilted and has begun to soften, about 7 minutes.

Stir in the wild rice blend and chicken broth and raise the heat to medium-high. Bring to a simmer, then reduce the heat to medium-low, cover, and cook until the rice is tender but still a bit chewy, about 45 minutes. Stir in the cream and cook until just heated through. Ladle the soup into bowls, sprinkle with the parsley, and serve.

WINE SUGGESTION: A DRY WHITE FROM PIEDMONT, SUCH AS GAVI DI GAVI OR ARNEIS ROERO

This nourishing soup is a specialty from the mountains of northwestern Tuscany. Here I use the robust dark green, lacinato kale, in place of the usual smoked pancetta for a hearty vegetarian version.

vegetable & farro soup

1½ cups (8 oz/250 g) freshly shelled borlotti (cranberry) beans

2 cloves garlic, crushed flat but left whole

1 fresh sprig *each* rosemary, thyme, and sage

1 bay leaf

5 tablespoons (3 fl oz/80 ml) extra-virgin olive oil, plus more for drizzling

2 carrots, peeled and finely chopped

1 rib celery, finely chopped

1 small yellow onion, finely chopped

2 tablespoons minced fresh herbs, such as parsley, rosemary, and thyme

1 small bunch lacinato (dinosaur) kale, tough bottom stems removed, leaves coarsely shredded

½ cup (4 oz/125 g) tomato purée

Fine sea salt

1 small fresh hot chile, minced

1 cup (8 fl oz/250 ml) chicken broth

1 cup (7 oz/220 g) *farro*, rinsed and drained

4 large fresh basil leaves, roughly chopped

Freshly grated *pecorino toscano* cheese

serves 4–6

In a large, heavy-bottomed saucepan, combine the beans, garlic, herb sprigs, bay leaf, and 2 tablespoons of the olive oil. Add water to cover by 1 inch (2.5 cm) and bring to a boil over high heat. Reduce the heat to medium-low and simmer gently until the beans are tender, about 30 minutes. Remove from the heat and discard the herb sprigs. Set aside and cover to keep warm.

In a soup pot, heat the remaining 3 tablespoons olive oil over medium-low heat. Stir in the carrots, celery, onion, and minced herbs and sauté until the onion is softened, 7–8 minutes. Stir in the kale and cook until wilted and just tender, 10–15 minutes. Stir in the tomato purée, 1 teaspoon salt, and the chile and raise the heat to medium. Add the chicken broth and 3 cups (24 fl oz/750 ml) water and bring to a boil.

Stir in the *farro* and the cooked beans with their liquid. Bring the soup to a boil, cover partially, and reduce the heat to medium-low. Simmer gently until the *farro* is tender but not mushy, about 40 minutes.

Sprinkle in the basil and remove from the heat. Let stand for about 5 minutes, then ladle into bowls, garnish with cheese and a drizzle of olive oil, and serve.

WINE SUGGESTION: A LOW-TANNIN RED, SUCH AS LANGHE ROSSO OR BARBERA D'ALBA

The bright flavors of this soup will shine through if served cold, but the truth is, I like it best hot. I make it mostly in late September, when farmers' markets are overflowing with ripe, sweet peppers.

roasted bell pepper soup with sourdough croutons

1½ lb (750 g) red bell peppers, seeded and cut into chunks

1½ lb (750 g) plum tomatoes, seeded and cut into chunks

2 yellow onions, cut into chunks

2 cloves garlic, halved

4 fresh thyme sprigs

5 large fresh basil leaves, shredded or torn

Fine sea salt and freshly ground black pepper

¼ cup (2 fl oz/60 ml) extra-virgin olive oil, plus 2 tablespoons

3 cups (24 fl oz/750 ml) vegetable broth

½ cup (4 fl oz/125 ml) heavy or light cream

4 slices sourdough baguette, about 1 inch (2.5 cm) thick

serves 4

Preheat the oven to 425°F (220°C). In a roasting pan, combine the peppers, tomatoes, onions, garlic, thyme sprigs, basil, 1 teaspoon salt, and a generous grinding of pepper. Drizzle the ¼ cup (2 fl oz/60 ml) olive oil over the vegetables and toss to coat. Roast, stirring every 15 minutes, until tender and browned in spots, 45–55 minutes.

Let the vegetables cool for 10 minutes. Remove the thyme sprigs. Transfer to a blender or food processor and add 1½ cups (12 fl oz/375 ml) of the broth. Process to a coarse purée, then pass through a fine-mesh sieve or food mill to remove the tomato and pepper skins. Transfer the purée to a saucepan and stir in the remaining 1½ cups (12 fl oz/375 ml) broth and the cream. Place over medium-low heat and cook until warmed through, about 10 minutes.

Meanwhile, in a frying pan, heat the 2 tablespoons olive oil over medium heat. Arrange the bread slices in the pan and cook until browned on the bottoms, about 3 minutes. Turn and brown on the second side, about 3 minutes longer.

Ladle the soup into bowls, top each with a sourdough crouton, and serve.

WINE SUGGESTION: PROSECCO, THE SPARKLING WHITE FROM THE VENETO

Roasting ordinary table grapes is a trick I learned from my friend Marie, who blogs at Proud Italian Cook. The hot oven softens the skins and intensifies the fruit's flavor. They pair perfectly with the rich Parmigiano-Reggiano cheese and toasted hazelnuts in this salad.

little gem salad with roasted grapes, parmigiano & hazelnuts

1 lb (500 g) red seedless grapes

4–6 tablespoons (2–3 fl oz/60–90 ml) extra-virgin olive oil

Fine sea salt and freshly ground black pepper

2 teaspoons Dijon mustard

2 teaspoons honey

1 teaspoon aged balsamic vinegar

2 heads Little Gem lettuce, leaves separated

1½ oz (45 g) Parmigiano-Reggiano cheese, shaved

2 tablespoons hazelnuts, lightly toasted, skinned, and coarsely chopped (see Cook's Note, page 62)

serves 6

Preheat the oven to 425°F (220°C).

Remove most of the grapes from their stems, but leave 2 or 3 clusters together. Spread all of the grapes out on a rimmed baking sheet and toss gently with 2 tablespoons of the olive oil. Season lightly with salt. Roast until the grapes are softened but still hold their shape, 10–15 minutes. Transfer the grapes to a bowl, and pour the accumulated juice from the baking sheet into a separate small bowl.

As the grapes cool, they will release more juice; add it to the small bowl. Whisk in the mustard, honey, and vinegar, and season with a pinch of salt and a few grindings of pepper. Whisk in 2–4 tablespoons olive oil, enough to achieve an emulsified dressing.

Place the lettuce in a deep serving platter and scatter the loose grapes on top. Drizzle the dressing over the salad, and sprinkle the cheese and hazelnuts on top. Garnish with the grape clusters and serve.

WINE SUGGESTION: PECORINO, A SOFT AND FRUITY WHITE FROM ABRUZZO AND LE MARCHE

Those pretty purple globes of flowers you see atop onion and garlic plants have a mild onion flavor and are a tasty addition to salads. Look for them at your local farmers' market, or replace them with snipped fresh chives.

tomato salad with basil vinaigrette

FOR THE VINAIGRETTE

1 cup (1 oz/30 g) lightly packed fresh purple basil leaves

1 small clove garlic, coarsely chopped

1 tablespoon red wine vinegar

1 tablespoon balsamic vinegar

Fine sea salt

⅓ cup (3 fl oz/80 ml) extra-virgin olive oil

1 lb (500 g) mixed heirloom tomatoes, cut into slices ¼ inch (6 mm) thick

1 cup (6 oz/185 g) cherry tomatoes, halved

1 tablespoon snipped onion flowers (see note)

Freshly ground black pepper

serves 4

To make the vinaigrette, in a food processor, combine the basil, garlic, vinegars, and ½ teaspoon salt and pulse until the basil is coarsely chopped. With the motor running, drizzle in the olive oil and process just until the vinaigrette is emulsified. Transfer to a small bowl or a glass jar and set aside.

Arrange the tomatoes on a serving platter and pour the vinaigrette over them (you may not need all of it). Sprinkle the onion flowers over the tomatoes, grind a little pepper over the top, and serve.

WINE SUGGESTION: CHIANTI CLASSICO OR OTHER SANGIOVESE-BASED RED

Although spinach salad is not a traditional Italian recipe, this particular version, with pickled shallots and pancetta, feels authentic, like a dish you might enjoy at lunch outdoors in a sunny piazza.

spinach salad with pickled shallot & pancetta

1 shallot, halved and thinly sliced

¼ cup (2 fl oz/60 ml) red wine vinegar

2 tablespoons sugar

¼ lb (125 g) pancetta, cut into ¼-inch (6-mm) dice

1 tablespoon extra-virgin olive oil

Fine sea salt and freshly ground black pepper

8 oz (250 g) baby spinach

serves 4

Put the shallot in a heatproof bowl. In a small saucepan over medium heat, combine the vinegar, sugar, and ¼ cup (2 fl oz/60 ml) water. Bring to a boil and simmer, stirring, until the sugar is dissolved. Pour the hot vinegar mixture over the shallot and let stand, uncovered at room temperature, for at least 30 minutes and up to 2 hours.

In a dry frying pan over medium heat, sauté the pancetta until crispy and the fat is rendered, about 10 minutes. Using a slotted spoon, transfer to paper towels to drain. Pour the hot fat into another heatproof bowl.

Strain the shallot, reserving the pickling liquid. Whisk ¼ cup (2 fl oz/60 ml) of the pickling liquid into the pancetta fat along with the olive oil, ½ teaspoon salt, and pepper to taste. Taste and adjust the seasoning with the pickling liquid, if needed.

Place the spinach in a large salad bowl and scatter the shallot over the top. Drizzle in the dressing and toss gently to coat. Sprinkle the pancetta on top and serve.

WINE SUGGESTION: A LIGHT RED, SUCH AS MONTEPULCIANO D'ABRUZZO

Around February, when I'm yearning for the fresh flavors of summer, I make this salad. The jewel tones of roasted beets, the citrusy tang of the oranges, and the bite of red onion are a wonderful antidote to the winter doldrums.

beets with blood oranges & fennel

1 large fennel bulb, cored and cut crosswise into slices about ½ inch (12 mm) thick, plus 1 tablespoon chopped fennel fronds

2 tablespoons extra-virgin olive oil

Fine sea salt and freshly ground black pepper

1 lb (500 g) beets, peeled and quartered

FOR THE VINAIGRETTE

2 tablespoons fresh blood orange juice

2 tablespoons red wine vinegar

2 tablespoons honey

Fine sea salt and freshly ground black pepper

¼ cup (2 fl oz/60 ml) extra-virgin olive oil

3 blood oranges, peel and pith removed, cut crosswise into slices ¼ inch (6 mm) thick

¼ red onion, thinly sliced

serves 4–6

Preheat the oven to 400°F (200°C). In a roasting pan, toss the fennel bulb slices with 1 tablespoon of the olive oil and sprinkle with salt and pepper. Cover with aluminum foil and roast for 20 minutes. Remove the foil and roast until tender and browned, about 20 minutes longer.

In a separate roasting pan, toss the beets with the remaining 1 tablespoon olive oil and sprinkle with salt and pepper. Cover with aluminum foil and roast until tender, about 30 minutes.

Meanwhile, make the vinaigrette: In a bowl, whisk together the orange juice, vinegar, honey, 1 teaspoon salt, and pepper to taste. Drizzle in the olive oil, whisking constantly until emulsified.

Transfer the beets and fennel to a bowl. Drizzle with 2–3 tablespoons of the vinaigrette and toss gently to coat.

Arrange the orange slices on a serving platter and scatter the onion on top. Drizzle with 2–3 tablespoons of the vinaigrette and sprinkle with salt and pepper. Spoon the beets and fennel on top and drizzle the remaining vinaigrette over them. Sprinkle with the chopped fennel fronds and serve.

WINE SUGGESTION: A CRISP, DRY WHITE, SUCH AS GRILLO OR INZOLIA FROM SICILY

My sister, Maria, is an excellent improvisational cook. Once while she and her family were visiting, she created this colorful and savory salad, which we served as a second course after pasta.

tricolor salad with bresaola & ubriaco cheese

1 head butter lettuce, leaves separated and torn into large pieces

1 head radicchio di Chioggia, cored, leaves torn into large pieces

About 4 oz (125 g) wild or baby arugula

1 cup (6 oz/185 g) drained jarred or canned artichoke hearts, halved or quartered

6 very thin slices bresaola (air-cured beef), cut crosswise into thin strips

⅓ cup (1½ oz/45 g) sliced almonds

1½ oz (45 g) crumbled *Ubriaco* cheese, plus more for garnish

3–4 tablespoons extra-virgin olive oil

2 tablespoons aged balsamic vinegar or fresh lemon juice

Fine sea salt and freshly ground black pepper

serves 6–8

In a large serving bowl, combine the lettuce, radicchio, and arugula and toss to mix. Add the artichoke hearts, bresaola, almonds, and cheese and toss gently. Drizzle just enough of the olive oil over the salad to thoroughly coat but not saturate the greens. Sprinkle with the vinegar and season with salt and pepper. Toss again gently.

Garnish with a few more crumbles of cheese and serve.

WINE SUGGESTION: A LIGHT RED, SUCH AS MONTEPULCIANO D'ABRUZZO, OR A REFRESHING ROSÉ, SUCH AS CERASUOLO

The delicate green of butter lettuce and the blue-white crumbles of Gorgonzola call to mind winter's pale light, while toasted hazelnuts add a warming touch to this Piedmont-inspired salad.

butter lettuce with gorgonzola & dates

FOR THE VINAIGRETTE

3 tablespoons hazelnut oil

1 tablespoon balsamic vinegar

Fine sea salt and freshly ground black pepper

1 head butter lettuce, leaves torn into large pieces

3 pitted Medjool dates, cut into small pieces

3 oz (90 g) Gorgonzola *dolce,* crumbled

¼ red onion, thinly sliced

2 tablespoons hazelnuts, lightly toasted, skinned, and coarsely chopped (see Cook's Note)

serves 4

To make the vinaigrette, in a small bowl, whisk together the oil, vinegar, ¼ teaspoon salt, and a grinding of pepper.

Place the lettuce in a large salad bowl. Scatter the dates, Gorgonzola, and onion over the lettuce. Pour the vinaigrette over the salad and toss gently to coat thoroughly. Sprinkle the hazelnuts over the top and serve right away.

COOK'S NOTE: To toast hazelnuts, preheat the oven to 350°F (180°C). Place the shelled nuts on a rimmed baking sheet and bake until golden brown and fragrant, about 10 minutes. Wrap the hot hazelnuts in a clean kitchen towel and let stand for 1 minute, then roll the nuts in the towel between your palms to rub off the skins (not all the skins will come off, which is fine).

WINE SUGGESTION: NERO D'AVOLA, SICILY'S GREAT RED

My father grew arugula in our backyard garden when I was growing up. As a kid, I avoided the peppery greens whenever possible; now I eat them every chance I can get. *Sovrano*, a lovely buffalo milk grating cheese, is worth seeking out.

arugula with figs, honey & sovrano cheese

FOR THE DRESSING

2 tablespoons extra-virgin olive oil

Juice of 1 small lemon

2 teaspoons balsamic vinegar

2 tablespoons flavorful honey, such as wildflower or summer thistle

Fine sea salt and freshly ground black pepper

8 fresh Mission figs, quartered lengthwise

8 oz (250 g) wild or baby arugula leaves, tough stems removed

2 tablespoons shaved *Sovrano* or Parmigiano-Reggiano cheese

serves 4

To make the dressing, in a small bowl, whisk together the olive oil, lemon juice, vinegar, honey, 1 teaspoon salt, and pepper to taste. Let stand for about 10 minutes to allow the flavors to develop.

Place the figs in a small bowl. Drizzle in 2 tablespoons of the dressing and toss gently to coat.

Place the arugula leaves in a large salad bowl and pour the remaining dressing over them. Toss gently until the leaves are thoroughly coated. Arrange the figs on top of the greens, scatter the cheese on top, and serve.

WINE SUGGESTION: A WHITE FROM NORTHEASTERN ITALY, SUCH AS COLLI ORIENTALI DEL FRIULI

Osteria Morini, on the waterfront in Washington, D.C., serves a similar salad in winter. It's one of my favorites—the bracing fruit and rich cheese complement one another beautifully and provide the perfect antidote to the chilly mid-Atlantic weather.

grapefruit, fennel & burrata salad

1 Ruby grapefruit

1 white grapefruit

1 small fennel bulb, halved, cored, and cut lengthwise into very thin slices, plus 1 tablespoon chopped fennel fronds

1–2 tablespoons honey

Fine sea salt and freshly ground black pepper

2 tablespoons extra-virgin olive oil

1 small ball (4 oz/125 g) *burrata* cheese

serves 4

Set a colander over a bowl. Using a serrated knife, cut off the tops and bottoms of the grapefruits. Then slice from top to bottom to remove the rind and bitter white pith. Holding the grapefruit over the colander, cut the segments of fruit from the membranes, letting the segments fall into the colander. Let drain for about 5 minutes, then transfer the segments to a separate bowl and add the fennel bulb slices.

Transfer 2 tablespoons of the grapefruit juice to a small bowl and whisk in 1–2 tablespoons honey, depending on how sweet the juice is. Season with ½ teaspoon salt and a few grindings of pepper. Whisk in the olive oil until the dressing is emulsified.

Drizzle the dressing over the grapefruit and fennel and toss gently to combine. Spoon the salad onto a serving plate or shallow bowl.

Slice the cheese in half and scoop out the creamy filling with a spoon. Chop the "skin," or exterior, into small pieces. Scatter the filling and chopped pieces over the salad. Sprinkle the fennel fronds on top and season with a grinding of pepper. Serve right away.

WINE SUGGESTION: PECORINO, A SOFT AND FRUITY WHITE FROM ABRUZZO AND LE MARCHE

The summer that my husband and I started dating, I wooed him with the bumper crop of beans—green, purple, and yellow—from my small garden. We enjoyed them in this salad and in other guises all summer long and, more than twenty years later, we still do.

string bean salad with ricotta salata & lemon

½ lb (250 g) yellow (wax) beans, stem ends removed

½ lb (250 g) green beans, stem ends removed

1 large ripe tomato, cut into bite-size chunks

2–3 tablespoons lemon-infused olive oil or extra-virgin olive oil

Finely grated zest of ½ lemon

Fine sea salt and freshly ground black pepper

8 fresh basil leaves, preferably 4 green and 4 purple, finely shredded

2 tablespoons crumbled ricotta *salata* cheese

serves 4

Place a steamer basket in a large saucepan and fill the pan with water up to but not touching the bottom of the basket. Bring the water to a boil over high heat. Add the beans to the basket, cover, and steam until just tender-crisp, 4–5 minutes. The green beans should be bright green.

Transfer the beans to a large salad bowl. Add the tomato, sprinkle with the olive oil and lemon zest, and toss to mix. Add ¼ teaspoon salt, a small grinding of pepper, the basil ribbons, and the cheese, toss again, and serve.

WINE SUGGESTION: PINOT GRIGIO, THE CRISP AND ACIDIC WHITE FROM ALTO ADIGE

Seafood salads are a staple on menus along the Adriatic coast of Abruzzo, where I spent my summers as a girl and enjoyed the endless combinations of cuttlefish, calamari, shrimp, mussels, and tiny clams. This version is simple but delivers loads of flavor.

citrusy shrimp & calamari salad

Juice of 2 lemons (about ¼ cup/2 fl oz/60 ml)

2 tablespoons red wine vinegar

1 tablespoon Dijon mustard

1 clove garlic, crushed in a garlic press

Fine sea salt and freshly ground black pepper

1 lb (500 g) cleaned calamari bodies and tentacles

1 lb (500 g) large shrimp, peeled and deveined

¼ cup (1 oz/30 g) thinly sliced red onion

1 small fresh hot chile, thinly sliced crosswise, or a generous pinch of red pepper flakes

2 tablespoons coarsely chopped fresh flat-leaf parsley

2 fresh bay leaves, or 4 dried bay leaves

3 long strips lemon zest

Crusty bread for serving

serves 4–6

In a small bowl, whisk together the lemon juice, vinegar, mustard, garlic, 1 teaspoon salt, and a generous grinding of pepper. Set aside.

Bring a large pot of water to a boil over high heat. Cut the calamari bodies into rings ¾ inch (2 cm) thick. Add the calamari rings and tentacles to the boiling water and cook for 2 minutes. Add the shrimp and cook until all the seafood is opaque throughout but still tender, about 4 minutes longer. Drain well and transfer to a bowl.

Pour the dressing over the seafood. It will seem like a lot, but the ample amount is necessary for marinating. Add the onion, chile, and parsley and stir to mix well. Tuck in the bay leaves and lemon zest, cover, and refrigerate until well chilled, at least 2 hours. Stir occasionally so that all the pieces marinate thoroughly.

Discard the lemon zest and the bay leaves. Divide the salad among small plates and serve with the bread on the side for sopping up the juices.

WINE SUGGESTION: A CRISP WHITE, SUCH AS GRILLO FROM SICILY OR VERMENTINO FROM SARDINIA

There are countless versions of this classic Tuscan salad, as *panzanella* is one of those versatile dishes that beg to be played with—try adding oil-cured tuna, hard-boiled eggs, cucumber, or baby arugula. Just keep it simple and fresh.

tuscan bread salad with caper dressing

FOR THE DRESSING

2 tablespoons red wine vinegar

1 tablespoon balsamic vinegar

1 teaspoon Dijon mustard

1 clove garlic, minced

Fine sea salt and freshly ground black pepper

¼ cup (2 fl oz/60 ml) extra-virgin olive oil

1 tablespoon capers, minced

¼ lb (4 oz/125 g) green beans

2 large ripe tomatoes

½ cup (2½ oz/75 g) pitted Gaeta olives, halved

4 oz (125 g) fresh mozzarella, cut into ½-inch (12-mm) dice

⅓ cup (1½ oz/45 g) thinly sliced red onion

6 thick slices day-old country bread, crusts removed, lightly toasted

10 fresh mint leaves

5 large fresh basil leaves

Freshly grated Parmigiano-Reggiano cheese for serving

serves 6–8

To make the dressing, in a bowl, whisk together the vinegars, mustard, garlic, ½ teaspoon salt, and a generous grinding of pepper. Drizzle in the olive oil, whisking constantly until emulsified. Stir in the capers and set aside.

Bring a pot of water to a boil over high heat. Cut the beans into 1-inch (2.5-cm) pieces and add to the boiling water. Cook until bright green and just tender-crisp, about 3 minutes. Drain in a colander and place under running cold water to stop the cooking. Drain again and transfer to a large salad bowl.

Cut the tomatoes into bite-size chunks and add to the bowl. Add the olives, mozzarella, and onion and toss to combine. Tear the bread into pieces and add to the bowl, then chop or tear the mint and basil leaves and scatter over the top. Pour the dressing over the salad and fold gently until all of the ingredients are well coated.

Cover and let the *panzanella* stand for 1 hour. Just before serving, toss once and garnish with the Parmigiano.

WINE SUGGESTION: A TUSCAN WHITE WITH GOOD ACIDITY, SUCH AS VERNACCIA DI SAN GIMIGNANO

Lentils are a staple ingredient in the hill towns of Umbria, where the most popular variety, prized for its delicate flavor and ability to hold its shape during cooking, is cultivated in the fields of Castelluccio.

lentil salad with lemon-rosemary vinaigrette

FOR THE VINAIGRETTE

Juice of 2 lemons (about ¼ cup/2 fl oz/60 ml)

1 tablespoon minced fresh rosemary

Fine sea salt

½ cup (4 fl oz/125 ml) extra-virgin olive oil

3 cups (1 lb/500 g) coarsely chopped carrots (from about 4 large carrots)

2 shallots, cut lengthwise into thin wedges

2 tablespoons extra-virgin olive oil

Fine sea salt and freshly ground black pepper

1½ cups (10½ oz/330 g) small brown lentils, preferably Castelluccio, or French green (Puy) lentils

1 bay leaf

1 clove garlic, crushed flat but left whole

serves 4–6

To make the vinaigrette, in a bowl, whisk together the lemon juice, rosemary, and 1 teaspoon salt. Slowly drizzle in the olive oil, whisking constantly until emulsified. Let stand at room temperature while you make the salad.

Preheat the oven to 425°F (220°C). Add the carrots and shallots to a large bowl, drizzle with the olive oil, and toss to coat. Season with ½ teaspoon salt and a grinding of pepper. Transfer to a large rimmed baking sheet and spread in a single layer. Roast until browned in spots and tender but not mushy, about 20 minutes. Remove from the oven and tent loosely with aluminum foil to keep warm.

Meanwhile, in a saucepan, combine the lentils, bay leaf, garlic, and 4 cups (32 fl oz/1 l) water and bring to a boil over medium-high heat. Reduce the heat to medium-low, cover, and cook at a gentle simmer until the lentils are almost tender but still slightly undercooked, 12–15 minutes. Stir in ¾ teaspoon salt, re-cover, and cook until the lentils are tender but still hold their shape, about 10 minutes longer. Drain the lentils in a colander placed in the sink. Discard the bay leaf and garlic.

Transfer the lentils to a large salad bowl and add the carrots and shallots. Pour the vinaigrette over the salad and toss gently to combine. Serve warm.

WINE SUGGESTION: PROSECCO, THE SPARKLING WHITE FROM THE VENETO

Farro, once an obscure ingredient harking from the Middle East and Tuscany, is now a globally popular grain that stars in everything from hearty stews to risotto-style dishes to salads like this crunchy winter mix.

farro salad with fennel, endive & hearts of palm

2 tablespoons fresh lemon juice

1 tablespoon red wine vinegar

1 clove garlic, minced

Fine sea salt and freshly ground black pepper

½ cup (4 fl oz/125 ml) extra-virgin olive oil

1½ cups (10½ oz/330 g) *farro*

½ fennel bulb, cored and finely diced

3 small ribs celery, finely diced

2 small heads Belgian endive, 1 red and 1 white, cut crosswise into slices ½ inch (12 mm) thick

1 cup (6 oz/185 g) drained jarred or canned hearts of palm, diced

¼ cup (⅓ oz/10 g) chopped fresh flat-leaf parsley

½ cup (2 oz/60 g) chopped toasted walnuts

serves 6

In a small bowl, whisk together the lemon juice, vinegar, garlic, 1 teaspoon salt, and a generous grinding of pepper. Drizzle in the olive oil, whisking constantly until emulsified. Set the dressing aside.

Rinse and drain the *farro*, then transfer to a large saucepan and add 3 cups (24 fl oz/750 ml) cold water. Stir in 1 teaspoon salt and bring to a boil over high heat. Reduce the heat to medium-low, cover partially, and simmer until the *farro* is tender but still chewy, about 20 minutes. Drain thoroughly and transfer to a large salad bowl.

Pour half of the dressing over the *farro* while still warm and toss gently to coat the grains well. Add the fennel, celery, endive, hearts of palm, and parsley. Pour over the remaining dressing and fold everything together gently until evenly distributed. Garnish with the walnuts and serve right away, or cover and refrigerate for 2–3 hours until completely chilled.

WINE SUGGESTION: A WHITE WITH GOOD ACIDITY, SUCH AS VERNACCIA DI SAN GIMIGNANO

pasta, risotto & pizza

There is no stand-in for a simple sauce made with fresh grated tomatoes, so I make this often in the summer. No one in my family complains—we know that once the season ends, it's farewell to fresh sauce until next year.

spaghetti with grated tomato sauce & ricotta

3 lb (1.5 kg) plum tomatoes

3 tablespoons extra-virgin olive oil

2 cloves garlic, crushed flat but left whole

Fine sea salt

5 large fresh basil leaves, torn into small pieces

1 lb (500 g) dried spaghetti

4 oz (125 g) ricotta *salata* cheese, crumbled

serves 4

Cut the tomatoes in half lengthwise and remove the seeds. Place a box grater in a large bowl and carefully grate the cut side of a tomato half against the large holes of the grater. You will be left with only the tomato skin in your hand. Repeat to seed and grate the remaining tomato halves. Discard the skins.

In a sauté pan over medium heat, warm the olive oil and garlic until the garlic begins to sizzle, about 2 minutes. Press the garlic with the back of a wooden spoon to release its aroma. Do not let the garlic brown or it will become bitter.

Slowly pour the grated tomatoes into the pan. Be careful, because the oil will spatter. Stir well and bring to a simmer. Add 1 teaspoon salt and cook, stirring from time to time, until the sauce has thickened, about 30 minutes. Remove from the heat, remove and discard the garlic, and stir in the basil.

While the sauce is cooking, bring a large pot of salted water to a boil over high heat. Add the spaghetti, stir once or twice, and cook until al dente, about 12 minutes or according to the package instructions. Drain well and return to the pot. Add about three-fourths of the sauce to the pot and toss to coat the strands thoroughly. Divide among 4 shallow bowls. Spoon some of the remaining sauce on top, garnish with the cheese, and serve.

WINE SUGGESTION: BARBERA D'ALBA, A MEDIUM-BODIED RED FROM PIEDMONT

Pasta al forno is one of those dishes that I never make the same way twice. I love to mix it up with different cheeses and vegetables or meat, sometimes adding tomato sauce and sometimes not. I created this version at the beach during a (thankfully) minor hurricane. While we waited out the storm, I played around in the kitchen.

baked ziti with eggplant & smoked scamorza

½ cup (4 fl oz/125 ml) extra-virgin olive oil

1 lb (500 g) eggplant, peeled (optional) and cubed

8 oz (250 g) shiitake mushrooms, stems removed, caps thinly sliced

Fine sea salt and freshly ground black pepper

2 cloves garlic, crushed flat but left whole

5 cups (35 oz/1.1 kg) canned diced tomatoes

5 fresh basil leaves, torn into small pieces

1 lb (500 g) dried ziti, penne, or other short, sturdy pasta

2 cups (8 oz/250 g) shredded smoked *scamorza* cheese

1 cup (4 oz/125 g) freshly grated Parmigiano-Reggiano cheese

serves 8

In a large frying pan, heat ¼ cup (2 fl oz/60 ml) of the olive oil over medium heat. Add the eggplant and mushrooms and stir to coat with the oil. Sprinkle in ¾ teaspoon salt and a generous grinding of pepper. Sauté until the vegetables are tender and browned in spots, about 20 minutes. Remove from the heat, cover to keep warm, and set aside.

In a large saucepan over medium heat, combine 3 tablespoons of the remaining olive oil and the garlic and warm until the garlic begins to sizzle, about 2 minutes. Press the garlic with the back of a wooden spoon to release its aroma. Do not let it brown or it will become bitter. Slowly pour the tomatoes into the pan. Be careful, because the oil and juice will spatter. Stir in ¾ teaspoon salt. Bring to a boil, then reduce the heat to medium-low and simmer until nicely thickened, about 30 minutes. Remove from the heat and stir in the basil. Cover the sauce to keep warm and set aside.

While the vegetables and tomato sauce are cooking, bring a large pot of salted water to a boil over high heat. Add the ziti and cook until al dente, about 11 minutes or according to the package directions. Drain, reserving about ½ cup (4 fl oz/125 ml) of the cooking water, then return to the pot. Add the eggplant and mushrooms, about two-thirds of the sauce, and the *scamorza* and toss gently but thoroughly. Add a splash or two of the pasta-cooking water to loosen the sauce, if needed.

Preheat the oven to 400°F (200°C). Coat a large baking dish with the remaining 1 tablespoon olive oil. Spoon the dressed pasta into the dish. Top with the remaining sauce and the Parmigiano. Bake, uncovered, until bubbly and browned on top, about 30 minutes. Serve hot.

WINE SUGGESTION: A FRUITY RED, SUCH AS DOLCETTO D'ALBA OR DOLCETTO DI DOGLIANI

Japanese sweet potatoes have purple skin, creamy white flesh, and a sweet, almost-floral flavor. They are starchier than other sweet potatoes, making them perfect for this twist on classic gnocchi. If you are unable to find them, substitute 1 lb (500 g) orange-fleshed sweet potatoes and 1 lb (500 g) russet potatoes.

white sweet potato gnocchi with hazelnut pesto

2 lb (1 kg) Japanese sweet potatoes

2 cups (10 oz/315 g) unbleached all-purpose flour, plus more for dusting

1 large egg

Fine sea salt

1 cup (5 oz/155 g) toasted and skinned hazelnuts (see Cook's Note, page 62)

2 cups (2 oz/60 g) fresh flat-leaf parsley leaves

1 teaspoon finely grated lemon zest

½ cup (4 fl oz/125 ml) extra-virgin olive oil, plus more if needed

2 tablespoons hazelnut oil (optional)

½ cup (2 oz/60 g) freshly grated Parmigiano-Reggiano cheese, plus more for serving

serves 8

Put the sweet potatoes in a large pot and add water to cover by 2 inches (5 cm). Bring to a boil over high heat, then reduce the heat to medium-high and cook until tender, about 30 minutes. Drain well. When cool enough to handle, peel the potatoes and cut in half.

Press the potatoes through a potato ricer directly onto a lightly floured work surface to form an airy mound. Let cool slightly. Sprinkle 1¾ cups (8½ oz/265 g) of the flour around the mound. Make a well in the mound and add the egg and ¾ teaspoon salt. Using a fork, whisk the egg and begin to incorporate the potatoes, eventually incorporating the flour. Use a dough scraper to gather up any sticky bits of dough. Sprinkle the remaining ¼ cup (1½ oz/45 g) flour over the dough and very lightly knead until it forms a soft, shaggy ball. It should feel slightly tacky but not sticky. Gently move it to the side and cover with a kitchen towel.

Dust a work surface and 2 rimmed baking sheets with flour. Cut off a tangerine-sized piece of dough and gently roll into a rope about ¾ inch (2 cm) in diameter. Cut into 1-inch (2.5-cm) lengths. Roll each gnocchi down the curved tines of a fork or down the length of a gnocchi board to create an indentation on one side and grooves on the other. Place on a prepared baking sheet. Repeat with the remaining dough. You should have 150–175 gnocchi. If not cooking them right away, place the baking sheets in the freezer until the gnocchi are firm, at least 1 hour. Then transfer to airtight containers and freeze for up to 1 month. Cook directly from the freezer.

Bring a large pot of salted water to a boil over high heat. In a food processor, combine the hazelnuts, parsley, lemon zest, and 1 teaspoon salt. Pulse to break up the nuts and parsley leaves. With the motor running, drizzle in the olive oil and hazelnut oil, if using, until a coarse paste forms. Add more olive oil, if needed, to achieve a thick, pourable consistency. Scrape the pesto into a bowl and stir in the cheese. Spoon a little of the pesto into a warmed large serving bowl.

Add half of the gnocchi to the boiling water and cook until soft and fluffy but cooked through, 3–5 minutes. Using a skimmer, transfer them to the serving bowl and toss gently with the pesto, adding a splash of the cooking water to loosen the sauce, if needed. Cover to keep warm. Repeat to cook the remaining gnocchi and transfer to the bowl. Spoon on more pesto and toss gently (reserve any leftover pesto to toss with spaghetti). Sprinkle with a little cheese and serve.

WINE SUGGESTION: VALPOLICELLA RIPASSO, A FRUITY, COMPLEX RED FROM THE AREA NEAR THE NORTHERN CITY OF VERONA

I grew up on my mother's spinach *lasagne alla Bolognese*, a baked concoction of rich meat sauce, gooey mozzarella, and homemade spinach pasta. When short on time, I make this version, in which the ingredients are tossed together instead of layered.

free-form spinach lasagne with sausage

1 oz (30 g) dried porcini mushrooms, steeped in 1 cup (8 fl oz/250 ml) boiling water for 30 minutes

1 tablespoon unsalted butter

1 tablespoon extra-virgin olive oil, plus more for greasing

1 small yellow onion, finely chopped

1 can (28 oz/875 g) diced tomatoes

Fine sea salt

¼ cup (2 fl oz/60 ml) heavy cream

1 lb (500 g) sweet Italian sausage, removed from its casing

Spinach Pasta Dough (page 209), or 1 lb (500 g) fresh spinach pasta sheets

4 oz (125 g) fontina cheese, shredded

1 cup (4 oz/125 g) freshly grated Parmigiano-Reggiano cheese

serves 6

Drain the porcini, reserving the liquid. Chop the mushrooms and set aside. Strain the mushroom broth into a clean bowl through a fine-mesh sieve lined with a damp paper towel. Set aside.

In a saucepan over medium-low heat, melt the butter with the olive oil. When the butter is sizzling, add the onion and sauté until it has begun to soften, about 5 minutes. Pour in the tomatoes and season with ½ teaspoon salt. Simmer gently, uncovered, stirring from time to time, until the tomatoes have thickened, 25–30 minutes. Remove from the heat and stir in the cream. Cover the sauce to keep warm and set aside.

Put the sausage in a large frying pan over medium heat and cook, using a wooden spoon to break up any large chunks and stirring from time to time, until all of the sausage is lightly browned, about 20 minutes. Add the porcini and raise the heat to medium-high. Pour in the reserved porcini broth and simmer briskly until most of the liquid has been absorbed, about 5 minutes. Remove from the heat.

Preheat the oven to 375°F (190°C). Bring a large pot of salted water to a boil over high heat. Place a large bowl of ice water near the stove. Add the spinach noodles to the boiling water and cook for 1–2 minutes to soften them (they should not be fully cooked). Using a large strainer, transfer the noodles to the bowl of ice water. Stir for a minute or two, then drain well in a colander placed in the sink.

Spoon about 1 cup (8 fl oz/250 ml) of the tomato sauce into a large bowl. Slide in the noodles and toss gently until thoroughly coated with the sauce. Add the sausage mixture, a few more spoonfuls of sauce, the fontina, and ¾ cup (3 oz/90 g) of the Parmigiano. Lightly oil a 9-by-13-inch (23-by-33-cm) baking dish. Spoon in the lasagne mixture and sprinkle with the remaining Parmigiano. Bake, uncovered, until bubbly and browned on top, about 30 minutes. Let rest for 5 minutes, then serve hot.

WINE SUGGESTION: A ROBUST RED, SUCH AS SAGRANTINO DI MONTEFALCO FROM UMBRIA

Recently, I was cooking a batch of my mother's caramelized onions when it struck me that they'd be delicious tossed with *bucatini*. I added some pancetta to the mix and a new sauce was born.

bucatini with caramelized onions & pancetta

½ lb (250 g) pancetta, cut into ¼-inch (6-mm) dice

2 tablespoons extra-virgin olive oil

2½ lb (1.25 kg) red or yellow onions, or a mix of both, halved and very thinly sliced lengthwise

1 teaspoon minced fresh oregano

Fine sea salt and freshly ground black pepper

1 lb (500 g) dried *bucatini* or *perciatelli*

½ cup (4 fl oz/125 ml) dry white wine

½ cup (2 oz/60 g) freshly grated *pecorino romano* cheese, plus more for serving

serves 4

In a large frying pan over medium-low heat, sauté the pancetta until lightly crisped and a little of the fat is rendered, about 10 minutes. Using a slotted spoon, transfer to paper towels to drain. Set aside.

Add the olive oil to the pan and pile in the onions. Using tongs or a wooden spoon, gently toss the onions to coat them as much as you can with the fat. Cover the pan and cook, still over medium-low heat, until the onions are well wilted, 15–20 minutes. Add the oregano, 1 teaspoon salt, and a generous grinding of pepper and cook, uncovered, until golden brown, creamy, and greatly reduced in volume, about 30 minutes. Stir from time to time to prevent scorching.

Meanwhile, bring a large pot of salted water to a boil over high heat. Add the *bucatini*, stir, and cook until al dente, about 11 minutes or according to the package directions. Drain, reserving about ½ cup (4 fl oz/125 ml) of the cooking water.

Raise the heat under the onions to medium-high, pour in the wine, and stir to scrape up any browned bits from the pan bottom. Let it bubble for a minute, then add the reserved pancetta. Transfer the pasta to the pan and toss gently to combine. Add a splash or two of the pasta-cooking water to loosen the sauce, if needed. Sprinkle in the cheese and toss again. Divide among 4 shallow bowls and serve, passing additional cheese at the table.

WINE SUGGESTION: PECORINO, A SOFT WHITE FROM ABRUZZO OR LE MARCHE

Years ago while visiting friends in Ascoli Piceno, we ventured to a restaurant in the hills to enjoy noodles tossed with delicate zucchini blossoms. This is one of my favorite variations of that dish, with toothsome *cavatelli* and shavings of *grana* cheese.

cavatelli with zucchini blossoms

Fine sea salt and freshly ground black pepper

4 tablespoons (2 fl oz/60 ml) extra-virgin olive oil

2 medium zucchini, cut into large dice (about 2 cups/ 8 oz/250 g)

1 clove garlic, minced

12 zucchini blossoms, cut crosswise into thin slices

Zest of 1 lemon

Juice of ½ lemon

1 tablespoon finely chopped fresh basil

1 tablespoon finely chopped fresh flat-leaf parsley

1 lb (500 g) dried *cavatelli* or other short, sturdy pasta

½ cup (2 oz/60 g) shaved *grana padano* or Parmigiano-Reggiano cheese

serves 4

Bring a large pot of salted water to a boil over high heat.

In a large frying pan, heat 2 tablespoons of the olive oil over medium-high heat. When the oil is shimmering, add the zucchini and cook, without stirring, until the pieces are well browned on the bottom, about 5 minutes. Stir gently and cook until browned on all sides, about 3 minutes longer.

Reduce the heat to medium-low and add the garlic, squash blossoms, and lemon zest. Stir very gently to coat the blossoms with the oil, then add the lemon juice, 1 teaspoon salt, and a generous grinding of pepper. Remove from the heat and stir in the basil and parsley. Cover the sauce to keep warm and set aside.

Add the *cavatelli* to the boiling water, stir once or twice, and cook until al dente, about 10 minutes or according to the package directions. Drain, reserving about ½ cup (4 fl oz/125 ml) of the cooking water. Transfer the pasta to the pan with the sauce. Using tongs or a pasta fork, toss very gently to combine. Add a splash or two of the pasta-cooking water to loosen the sauce, if needed. Divide among shallow bowls, garnish with the cheese, and serve.

WINE SUGGESTION: PECORINO, A SOFT WHITE FROM ABRUZZO OR LE MARCHE

This recipe combines the sweetness of summer squash with the smokiness of *speck*. It is also gorgeous to look at: strands of thin spaghettini intertwined with bright green and yellow ribbons of squash and rosy flecks of ham.

spaghettini with summer squash & crispy speck

Fine sea salt and freshly ground black pepper

2 tablespoons extra-virgin olive oil

4 oz (125 g) Italian *speck*, cut into small dice

3 cloves garlic, very thinly sliced

1 lb (500 g) mixed zucchini and yellow summer squash, sliced very thinly lengthwise using a mandoline or vegetable peeler, then cut into thin strips

2 tablespoons finely shredded fresh basil

1 lb (500 g) dried spaghettini

½ cup (2 oz/60 g) freshly grated Parmigiano-Reggiano cheese

serves 4–6

Bring a large pot of salted water to a boil over high heat.

In a large frying pan over medium heat, combine the olive oil and *speck* and sauté until the *speck* is crispy, about 7 minutes. Add the garlic and sauté until it just begins to turn golden, about 3 minutes.

Add the squash and toss well to coat the strands with the oil. Season with ¼ teaspoon salt and a generous grinding of pepper. Raise the heat to medium-high and cook until the squash is just tender, 3–4 minutes. Stir in the basil and remove from the heat. Cover the sauce to keep warm and set aside.

Add the spaghettini to the boiling water, stir, and cook until al dente, about 9 minutes or according to the package directions. Drain, reserving about ½ cup (4 fl oz/125 ml) of the cooking water. Transfer the pasta to the pan with the sauce. Using tongs or a pasta fork, toss gently to combine. Add a splash or two of the pasta-cooking water to loosen the sauce, if needed. Sprinkle in the cheese and toss again. Season with salt and pepper. Divide among shallow bowls, spoon any remaining sauce on top, and serve.

WINE SUGGESTION: A SMOKY RED, SUCH AS DOLCETTO D'ALBA, OR A RICH WHITE, SUCH AS FALANGHINA OR FIANO DI AVELLINO

Skiing in the Dolomites is definitely on my bucket list. Until then, I satisfy myself with this northern Italian ragù, rich and savory and spiked with rosemary, bay leaves, and juniper berries.

tagliatelle with juniper-spiced short rib ragù

3 tablespoons vegetable oil

3½ lb (1.75 kg) bone-in beef short ribs

Fine sea salt and freshly ground black pepper

1 large yellow onion, diced

3 carrots, peeled and finely diced

3 ribs celery, finely diced

3 cloves garlic, minced

1 tablespoon minced fresh rosemary

2 bay leaves

⅓ cup (½ oz/15 g) minced fresh flat-leaf parsley

1½ cups (12 fl oz/375 ml) Basic Tomato Sauce (page 209) or canned diced tomatoes, with juice

1 bottle (750 ml) Sangiovese or other dry red wine

1 cup (8 fl oz/250 ml) chicken broth, preferably homemade (page 209)

1 teaspoon juniper berries

1 teaspoon peppercorns

2 recipes Basic Egg Pasta Dough (page 208), cut into tagliatelle, or 2 lb (1 kg) dried fettuccine

Freshly grated Parmigiano-Reggiano cheese for serving

serves 8–10

In a large, heavy-bottomed pot, heat the oil over medium heat. Add as many ribs as will fit without crowding the pot and season with salt and pepper. Brown the ribs on both sides, about 4 minutes on each side. Transfer to a platter. Repeat to brown the remaining ribs. Discard all but 2 tablespoons of the fat.

Reduce the heat to medium-low, add the onion, carrots, celery, and garlic, and stir to coat. Add the rosemary, bay leaves, and half of the parsley. Cook, stirring often, until the vegetables are softened, 8–10 minutes. Stir in ½ cup (4 fl oz/125 ml) of the tomato sauce, then return the ribs to the pot along with any accumulated juices. Pour in the wine and broth. Tie the juniper berries and peppercorns in a small piece of cheesecloth and add to the pot. Raise the heat to medium-high and bring to a boil. Reduce the heat to maintain a low simmer. Cover and cook very gently, stirring from time to time, until the meat is tender, about 2½ hours.

Transfer the meat to a cutting board. Remove and discard the cheesecloth bundle and bay leaves. Add the remaining 1 cup (8 fl oz/250 ml) tomato sauce and raise the heat to medium-high. Bring to a boil, reduce the heat to medium, and simmer until thickened, about 20 minutes. Remove the meat from the bones, discarding the bones. Shred or chop the meat coarsely, return to the pot, and cook until heated through, about 10 minutes. Turn off the heat, stir in the remaining parsley, and cover.

Meanwhile, bring a large pot of salted water to a boil over high heat. If using fresh pasta, add to the pot and stir to prevent sticking. Cook until al dente, 2–5 minutes. If using dried pasta, cook until al dente according to the package directions. Drain, reserving about ½ cup (4 fl oz/125 ml) of the cooking water. Return the pasta to the pot and spoon some of the ragù over it. Toss gently, coating the pasta well. Add a splash or two of the pasta-cooking water to loosen the sauce, if needed. Divide among shallow bowls and spoon more ragù on top. Sprinkle with cheese and serve.

WINE SUGGESTION: BARBARESCO OR BARBERA, TWO FINE MEDIUM-BODIED REDS FROM PIEDMONT

I never thought I'd be able to make this dish, which hails from the Italian countryside, in my own kitchen, but happily, nettles are now available at many farmers' markets come spring.

orecchiette with butter-braised nettles

12 oz (375 g) stinging nettles

Fine sea salt

2 tablespoons unsalted butter

2 tablespoons extra-virgin olive oil

3 cloves garlic, finely chopped

1 small fresh hot chile, minced, or a generous pinch of red pepper flakes

1 lb (500 g) dried orecchiette or other short, sturdy pasta

¾ cup (3 oz/90 g) freshly grated *pecorino romano* cheese

serves 4

Bring a large pot of water to a boil over high heat. Wearing gloves to prevent stinging, cut the tough stems off the nettles and rinse well. Using the gloves or tongs, place in the boiling water and blanch until wilted, 1–2 minutes. Drain and let cool, then chop coarsely. Fill the pot with fresh water. Salt generously and bring to a boil.

While the water is heating, in a large saucepan over medium heat, melt the butter with the olive oil. Add the garlic and chile and stir to coat with the fat. Reduce the heat to medium-low and cook until the garlic is fragrant, 1–2 minutes. Add the nettles and 1 teaspoon salt. Using tongs, toss the greens to coat well. Reduce the heat to low, cover, and cook gently, stirring from time to time, until the greens are tender, about 10 minutes.

Add the orecchiette to the boiling water and cook until al dente, about 8 minutes or according to the package directions. Drain, reserving about ½ cup (4 fl oz/125 ml) of the cooking water. Transfer the pasta to the pan with the greens and toss well to combine. Add a splash or two of the pasta-cooking water to loosen the sauce, if needed. Sprinkle half of the cheese over the pasta and toss again. Divide among 4 shallow bowls, garnish each serving with some of the remaining cheese, and serve.

WINE SUGGESTION: SOAVE, A DRY WHITE FROM THE VENETO

Italians love their bitter greens, whether served raw in salad, cooked in soup, or made the star of a savory filling for oversized ravioli. Use a mix of escarole, chicory, and dandelion greens, or try radicchio for an unusual but delicious riff.

ravioli with bitter greens & toasted walnut butter

FOR THE FILLING

1 lb (500 g) bitter greens, such as escarole, chicory, dandelion greens, and radicchio

2 tablespoons unsalted butter

1 tablespoon extra-virgin olive oil

2 shallots, diced

Fine sea salt and freshly ground black pepper

1 tablespoon fresh lemon juice

½ cup (4 oz/125 g) well-drained cow's milk ricotta

¼ lb (125 g) fresh mozzarella cheese, cut into small dice

Semolina flour for dusting

1 recipe Basic Egg Pasta Dough (page 208)

Kosher or sea salt

1½ cups (12 oz/375 g) salted butter

¾ cup (3 oz/90 g) coarsely chopped walnuts, lightly toasted

2 tablespoons fresh lemon juice

2 tablespoons minced fresh flat-leaf parsley

½ cup (2 oz/60 g) freshly grated *pecorino romano* cheese

serves 6–8

To make the filling, remove any cores and thick stems from the greens, then cut the leaves crosswise into thin shreds. Set aside. In a large frying pan, melt the butter with the olive oil over medium heat. When the butter starts to foam, add the shallots and cook, stirring often, until they start to soften, about 5 minutes. Add as many greens as you can by the handful and sprinkle with ¼ teaspoon salt. Cover and cook until they start to wilt, about 2 minutes. Uncover, stir, and add more greens. Repeat until you have added them all. Sprinkle with ¼ teaspoon salt and cook, uncovered, until the greens are quite wilted and soft, about 10 minutes longer. Sprinkle with the lemon juice and season lightly with pepper. Let cool briefly, then drain well, pressing out the liquid. Transfer to a cutting board and chop finely. In a bowl, combine the greens and cheeses and mix well. Cover and refrigerate until ready to use.

Dust a work surface and 2 rimmed baking sheets with semolina. Using a pasta machine, roll out the dough to ¹⁄₁₆-inch (2-mm) thickness (see page 208). You should have 4 long sheets. (If the sheets get too long and unwieldy, cut them in half crosswise and roll out the halves separately.) Lay a dough sheet on the floured surface with the longest edge facing you. Cover the other sheets with a kitchen towel. Spoon a scant 1 tablespoon filling along the center of the dough sheet at 3- to 3½-inch (7.5- to 9-cm) intervals and flatten the mounds slightly. Dip your finger in water and lightly moisten the edges of the dough and the area between the mounds. Lay a second dough sheet on top. Gently press down between the mounds to seal and remove any air bubbles. Using a pastry cutter, cut out large ravioli, each about a 3½ inches (9 cm) square. Alternately, use a large square or round cookie cutter or a ravioli cutter. Transfer to the prepared baking sheets, making sure the ravioli are not touching. Repeat with the remaining dough sheets and filling. You should have 24–28 large ravioli.

If cooking the ravioli right away, leave them on the prepared sheets. If cooking later in the day, place the baking sheets in the freezer and freeze until ready to cook. If not cooking them the same day, freeze until the ravioli are firm, at least 1 hour. Then transfer to airtight containers and freeze for up to 1 month.

Bring a large pot of salted water to a boil over high heat. Preheat the oven to 200°F (95°C). In a large saucepan, melt the butter over medium heat. When it begins to foam, swirl the pan and cook, watching carefully, until it begins to brown. Remove from the heat and swirl the pan if necessary to prevent the butter from browning too quickly. Return the pan to low heat and stir in the walnuts and lemon juice. Remove from the heat and cover. Spoon about one-third of the walnut butter into a large, shallow serving bowl or platter and place in the oven.

Add half of the ravioli to the boiling water and cook until al dente, 3–5 minutes. Using a skimmer, transfer them to the serving bowl. Spoon a little of the remaining walnut butter from the pan over them and sprinkle with a little parsley and cheese. Return the bowl to the oven. Repeat to cook the remaining ravioli and transfer to the bowl. Spoon the remaining walnut butter over them and sprinkle with the remaining parsley and cheese. Serve right away.

WINE SUGGESTION: ARNEIS ROERO, A FULL-BODIED WHITE FROM THE ROERO HILLS IN PIEDMONT

At my house, we have pasta for dinner a couple of times a week, dressed according to the season. In spring, when I can find fresh peas and sheep's milk ricotta, I make this wholesome sauce, which can be assembled in the time it takes to boil the pasta water.

fettuccine with peas, ricotta & prosciutto

Fine sea salt and freshly ground black pepper

2 tablespoons unsalted butter

1 tablespoon extra-virgin olive oil

1 small white onion, finely diced

2 cups (10 oz/315 g) fresh or thawed frozen peas

Zest of 2 lemons

1 lb (500 g) dried fettuccine

½ cup (4 oz/125 g) lightly packed fresh sheep's milk ricotta or well-drained cow's milk ricotta, at room temperature

4 thin slices prosciutto di Parma, cut into thin strips

½ cup (2 oz/60 g) freshly grated Parmigiano-Reggiano cheese

serves 4

Bring a large pot of salted water to a boil over high heat.

In a large frying pan over medium-low heat, melt the butter with the olive oil. When the butter has melted and begins to sizzle, add the onion and sauté until soft and translucent, 7–8 minutes. Add the peas, stir to coat thoroughly with the fat, and cook until just tender and no longer raw-tasting, about 7 minutes. Stir in ½ teaspoon salt, a generous grinding of pepper, and the lemon zest and remove from the heat. Cover the sauce to keep warm and set aside.

Add the fettuccine to the boiling water and cook until al dente, about 12 minutes or according to the package instructions. Drain, reserving about ½ cup (4 fl oz/125 ml) of the cooking water. Transfer the pasta to the pan with the sauce and toss gently to combine. Add a splash or two of the pasta-cooking water to loosen the sauce, if needed. Add the ricotta and prosciutto and toss gently to mix. Add the Parmigiano and toss gently again. Taste and adjust the seasoning. Divide among 4 shallow bowls and serve.

WINE SUGGESTION: VERDICCHIO DEI CASTELLI JESI (OR VERDICCHIO DI METALICA), A PLEASANTLY ACIDIC WHITE FROM LE MARCHE

In Linguria, there are as many recipes for this beguiling green sauce as there are cooks. In recent years, I've started to experiment with more and more variations. My family thinks that this one, with sweet pistachios and sharp pecorino, is the best.

trenette with pistachio pesto

Fine sea salt and freshly ground black pepper

2 cups (2 oz/60 g) lightly packed fresh basil leaves

1 cup (1 oz/30 g) lightly packed fresh flat-leaf parsley leaves

½ cup (2 oz/60 g) roasted unsalted pistachios

1 clove garlic, coarsely chopped

½–¾ cup (4–6 fl oz/125–180 ml) extra-virgin olive oil

½ cup (2 oz/60 g) freshly grated *pecorino romano* cheese, plus more for serving

1 lb (500 g) dried *trenette* or linguine

serves 4

Bring a large pot of salted water to a boil over high heat.

In a food processor, combine the basil, parsley, pistachios, garlic, ¾ teaspoon salt, and a few grindings of pepper. Process just until the herb leaves and nuts are coarsely chopped, stopping to scrape down the sides of the bowl as needed. With the motor running, drizzle in just enough olive oil to achieve a thick sauce consistency. Scrape the pesto into a bowl and stir in the pecorino.

Add the *trenette* to the boiling water and cook until al dente, about 11 minutes or according to the package instructions. Drain, reserving about ½ cup (4 fl oz/ 125 ml) cooking water. Transfer the pasta to a serving bowl and spoon about three-fourths of the pesto over it. Using a large serving fork or pasta fork, gently toss the noodles with the pesto. Add a splash or two of the pasta-cooking water to loosen the sauce, if needed. Divide among 4 shallow bowls. Dollop a little of the remaining pesto on top of each serving, sprinkle with a little cheese, and serve. Pass additional cheese at the table.

WINE SUGGESTION: A LOW-TANNIN RED, SUCH AS BARBERA D'ASTI OR BARBERA D'ALBA

This is one of those wonderful improvised summer dishes that Italians toss together with whatever happens to be in the garden and pantry. It's perfect for a sultry evening, when the thought of preparing a cooked sauce seems like too much work.

whole-wheat penne with oil-cured tuna

1 lb (500 g) ripe plum tomatoes, peeled, seeded, and cut into ¼-inch (6-mm) dice

3 cans (2.8 oz/85 g *each*) imported Italian or Spanish tuna packed in olive oil, drained and flaked

2 imported Italian or Spanish anchovy fillets, chopped

2 shallots, finely chopped

1 clove garlic, crushed flat but left whole

2 tablespoons coarsely chopped fresh flat-leaf parsley

2 tablespoons coarsely chopped fresh basil

1 small fresh hot chile, minced, or a generous pinch of red pepper flakes

3 tablespoons extra-virgin olive oil, plus more for drizzling

1 tablespoon red wine vinegar

1 lb (500 g) dried whole-wheat pasta such as penne *rigate* or *cavatappi*

8 oz (250 g) fresh mozzarella cheese, cut into small dice

serves 4

In a large serving bowl, combine the tomatoes, tuna, anchovies, shallots, garlic, parsley, basil, and chile and stir gently to mix. Add the olive oil and vinegar and toss gently again to coat. Add a little more olive oil if the sauce seems dry. Let stand at room temperature for at least 30 minutes and up to 1 hour to allow the flavors to mingle. Remove the clove of garlic right before you toss the sauce with the cooked pasta.

Bring a large pot of salted water to a boil over high heat. Add the pasta and cook until al dente, about 9 minutes or according to the package instructions. Drain well, then transfer the hot pasta to the bowl with the sauce and toss gently to combine. Add the mozzarella and toss again. Drizzle in a little more olive oil to loosen the sauce a bit, if needed, and serve.

WINE SUGGESTION: A MINERALLY SICILIAN WHITE, SUCH AS ETNA BIANCO OR ETNA BIANCO SUPERIORE

For the best flavor, I prefer to cook shrimp with their shells (and heads) on, but on a busy weeknight, I am grateful for the ease of peeled, deveined shrimp. Look for wild shrimp, which have a better taste and texture than the imported farmed variety.

lumache with shrimp, tomatoes & garlic

Fine sea salt

3 tablespoons extra-virgin olive oil

3 cloves garlic, very thinly sliced

1 small fresh hot chile, minced, or a generous pinch of red pepper flakes

1 can (14½ oz/455 g) diced tomatoes

⅓ cup (3 fl oz/80 ml) dry white wine

1 lb (500 g) large or jumbo shrimp, peeled, deveined, and each cut crosswise into 3 pieces

2 tablespoons chopped fresh flat-leaf parsley

1 lb (500 g) dried *lumache*, *conchiglie*, or farfalle

serves 4

Bring a large pot of salted water to a boil over high heat.

In a large frying pan, combine the olive oil and garlic and cook over medium-low heat until the garlic is softened but not browned, 7–8 minutes. Stir in the chile and cook until fragrant, about 1 minute. Raise the heat to medium-high, add the tomatoes, and bring to a simmer. Reduce the heat to medium-low and cook until the tomatoes have thickened a little, about 5 minutes. Return the heat to medium-high, pour in the wine, and let it bubble for a minute or so. Add the shrimp, stir, and reduce the heat to medium. Cook just until the shrimp are opaque throughout, 4–5 minutes. Season with salt and sprinkle in the parsley.

Add the *lumache* to the boiling water, stir once or twice, and cook until al dente, about 11 minutes or according to the package instructions. Drain, reserving about ½ cup (4 fl oz/125 ml) of the cooking water. Transfer the pasta to the pan with the sauce and toss gently to combine. Add a splash or two of the pasta-cooking water to loosen the sauce, if needed. Divide among 4 shallow bowls, spoon any remaining sauce on top, and serve.

WINE SUGGESTION: A FULL-BODIED WHITE FROM CAMPANIA, SUCH AS FIANO DI AVELLINO OR GRECO DI TUFO

I was introduced to *farro* years ago at a wonderful restaurant in Lucca, where it was used in a hearty soup with beans. The grain's appealing chewy-tender texture and earthy flavor also make it perfect for this risotto-style dish.

risotto-style farro with porcini & pecorino

1 oz (30 g) dried porcini mushrooms, steeped in 1 cup (8 fl oz/250 ml) boiling water for 30 minutes

4 tablespoons (2 fl oz/60 ml) extra-virgin olive oil

1 clove garlic, crushed flat but left whole

1 lb (500 g) mixed fresh mushrooms, such as cremini, portobello, and shiitake, sliced

½ teaspoon chopped fresh thyme

1 large shallot, finely chopped

1½ cups (10½ oz/330 g) *farro*, rinsed and drained

⅓ cup (3 fl oz/80 ml) dry white wine

4 cups (32 fl oz/1 l) chicken broth, preferably homemade (page 209), heated to a simmer

1 tablespoon balsamic vinegar

½ cup (2 oz/60 g) freshly grated *pecorino romano* cheese, plus a handful of shaved pieces for garnish

serves 4–6

Drain the porcini, reserving the liquid. Chop the mushrooms and strain the broth into a clean bowl through a fine-mesh sieve lined with a damp paper towel. Set aside.

In a frying pan over medium heat, warm 2 tablespoons of the olive oil and the garlic. Add the fresh mushrooms and the porcini to the pan and toss gently to coat them with the fat. Sprinkle in the thyme and cook, stirring often, until the mushrooms are tender and a little browned, 10 minutes. Remove and discard the garlic and set aside.

In a large, heavy-bottomed sauté pan over medium-low heat, combine the remaining 2 tablespoons olive oil and the shallot and sauté until the shallot is softened, about 5 minutes. Add the *farro* and stir until well coated with the oil, about 2 minutes. Raise the heat to medium-high, pour in the wine and reserved porcini broth, and stir until the liquid has been absorbed. Reduce the heat to medium and add a ladleful or two of the hot chicken broth. Cook, stirring from time to time (you don't have to stir it constantly), until the broth has been absorbed. Continue to cook, adding broth as needed, until the *farro* is tender but still pleasantly chewy, 25–30 minutes total.

Stir in the vinegar and grated cheese. Spoon the *farrotto* into a serving bowl, scatter the shaved pecorino on top, and serve.

WINE SUGGESTION: CHIANTI CLASSICO OR OTHER SANGIOVESE-BASED TUSCAN RED

Lemon and asparagus are a classic pairing for spring risotto. Here, the addition of lemon zest intensifies the flavor and the cream makes the dish more luxurious. If you are lucky enough to live in a place where you can find wild asparagus, by all means use it. The thin, grassy stalks are just right for stirring into risotto.

creamy lemon risotto with asparagus

1 lb (500 g) asparagus, woody ends removed

1 tablespoon unsalted butter

1 tablespoon extra-virgin olive oil

1 shallot, finely chopped

3 fresh thyme sprigs

2 cups (14 oz/440 g) Arborio, Carnaroli, or other risotto rice

Fine sea salt and freshly ground black pepper

¼ cup (2 fl oz/60 ml) dry white wine

6 cups (48 fl oz/1.5 l) chicken broth, preferably homemade (page 209), heated to a simmer

2 teaspoons finely grated lemon zest, plus 2 tablespoons fresh lemon juice

½ cup (4 fl oz/125 ml) heavy cream

½ cup (2 oz/60 g) freshly grated Parmigiano-Reggiano cheese

2 tablespoons minced fresh flat-leaf parsley

serves 4

In a microwave-safe bowl, combine the asparagus and 2 tablespoons water. Cover loosely with plastic wrap and microwave on high until the spears are tender-crisp, about 2 minutes. Alternatively, place the asparagus in a steamer basket and set over a saucepan of simmering water. Cover and steam until the spears are tender-crisp, 3 to 4 minutes. Cut into 1-inch (2.5-cm) pieces and set aside.

In a large, heavy-bottomed sauté pan, melt the butter with the olive oil over medium heat. When the butter has melted, add the shallot and cook, stirring often, until starting to soften, about 5 minutes. Stir in the thyme sprigs and cook until the shallot is softened and translucent, about 3 minutes longer.

Add the rice and 1 teaspoon salt, stirring to coat the grains with the butter and oil. Raise the heat to medium-high, pour in the wine, and stir until absorbed. Reduce the heat to medium and add a ladleful of the hot broth. Cook, stirring often, until the broth is absorbed. Reduce the heat to medium-low if necessary to maintain a gentle simmer. Continue to cook the risotto, adding the broth a ladleful at a time and stirring until it is absorbed, until the rice is tender but still pleasantly chewy, about 20 minutes.

Stir in the reserved asparagus, lemon zest, cream, and cheese. Then stir in the lemon juice and a final ladleful of broth to achieve a creamy texture. The risotto should not be too stiff or too runny; it should mound softly on a spoon. Sprinkle with the parsley, season with pepper, and serve.

WINE SUGGESTION: A WELL-BALANCED WHITE, SUCH AS FIANO DI AVELLINO OR GRECO DI TUFO, BOTH FROM CAMPANIA

This richly flavored risotto, which features long-leaved, ruby-colored radicchio—a specialty of Verona—is my tribute to that beautiful city. For a red wine risotto, use valpolicella wine in place of the prosecco.

prosecco risotto with radicchio

1 tablespoon unsalted butter

1 tablespoon extra-virgin olive oil

1 large shallot, finely chopped

1½ cups (10½ oz/330 g) Arborio, Carnaroli, or other risotto rice

¾ cup (6 fl oz/180 ml) prosecco

6–7 cups (48–56 fl oz/ 1.5–1.75 l) chicken broth, preferably homemade (page 209), heated to a simmer

2 medium heads radicchio di Verona, cored and leaves shredded (about 8 cups/ 8 oz/250 g)

1 tablespoon aged balsamic vinegar

2 tablespoons mascarpone or heavy cream

½ cup (2 oz/60 g) freshly grated Parmigiano-Reggiano cheese

serves 4

In a large, heavy-bottomed sauté pan over medium-low heat, melt the butter with the olive oil. When the butter has melted and begins to sizzle, add the shallot and sauté until softened but not browned, 7–8 minutes. Add the rice and stir until the grains are translucent, about 2 minutes.

Raise the heat to medium-high, pour in the prosecco, and stir until absorbed. Add a ladleful or two of the hot broth, just enough to cover the rice. Reduce the heat to medium and simmer gently, stirring often, until the broth is nearly absorbed. Stir in another ladleful or two of broth and then add the radicchio. Continue to cook the risotto, adding broth as needed, until the rice is tender but still pleasantly chewy, about 30 minutes total.

Add a final ladleful of broth and the vinegar and stir for a minute or two longer. Remove from the heat and stir in the mascarpone and half of the Parmigiano. Ladle the risotto into shallow bowls, sprinkle a little of the remaining cheese over each serving, and serve.

WINE SUGGESTION: VALPOLICELLA CLASSICO, A LIGHT AND FRUITY RED FROM VERONA

Pizza al taglio translates to pizza by the slice, and in Rome it is a perennially popular street food. The pizzas are baked in large rectangular trays and sold by weight. Toppings can run the gamut, but my favorite combination is fresh spinach and olives.

roman-style pizza
with spinach & olives

3 tablespoons extra-virgin olive oil, plus more for greasing

1½ cups (10½ oz/330 g) canned diced tomatoes

2 cloves garlic, crushed flat but left whole

5 fresh basil leaves, shredded

Fine sea salt

6 oz (185 g) fresh spinach leaves

1 recipe Pizza Dough (page 208)

Semolina flour or unbleached all-purpose flour for dusting

12 oz (375 g) fresh mozzarella cheese, thinly sliced

⅓ cup (1½ oz/45 g) thinly sliced red onion

¾ cup (4 oz/125 g) pitted Gaeta or Kalamata olives, halved lengthwise

serves 4–6

Preheat the oven to 500°F (260°C). Lightly oil a 12-by-17-inch (30-by-43-cm) rimmed baking sheet and set aside.

In a bowl, stir together the tomatoes, garlic, basil, ¼ teaspoon salt, and 2 tablespoons of the olive oil. Let stand at room temperature for at least 30 minutes and up to 1 hour. Remove and discard the garlic.

In a large frying pan, heat the remaining 1 tablespoon olive oil over medium heat. Add the spinach and, using tongs, turn to coat the leaves with the oil. Sauté just until barely wilted, 3–4 minutes. Remove from the heat and set aside.

Using your hands or a rolling pin, roll and stretch out the pizza dough on a lightly floured work surface and fit it into the prepared pan. Spoon the raw tomato sauce over the top, leaving a 1-inch (2.5-cm) border. Arrange the mozzarella slices, onion, spinach, and olives on top of the sauce. Bake until the cheese is bubbly and the crust is golden brown and crisped around the edges, about 15 minutes. Let rest for 5 minutes, then cut into rectangles and serve hot.

WINE SUGGESTION: A SANGIOVESE-BASED RED FROM TUSCANY, SUCH AS CHIANTI CLASSICO, OR A NERO D'AVOLA FROM SICILY

There's no way a standard home oven can duplicate the searing heat of a wood-fired pizza oven. But the grill works beautifully! Once you get used to handling the dough on the grate, you'll see how easy it is to make these colorful pizzas. I like to set out a variety of toppings and let everyone choose their own.

individual grilled pizzas

Vegetable oil for greasing

Semolina flour or unbleached all-purpose flour for dusting

1 recipe Pizza Dough (page 208)

Extra-virgin olive oil for brushing and drizzling

3 cups (12 oz/375 g) shredded *Fontina Val d'Aosta, Cacio di Roma,* goat's milk Gouda, or other melting cheese

2 ripe summer tomatoes, thinly sliced

1 small red onion, halved and cut into paper-thin slices

1 cup (5 oz/155 g) pitted Gaeta or Kalamata olives, halved

2 cups (2 oz/60 g) wild or baby arugula

½ cup (¾ oz/20 g) finely shredded fresh basil

Fine sea salt

serves 4

Prepare a fire in a charcoal grill or preheat a gas grill to high. If using charcoal, spread the hot coals across one half of the bottom of the grill and leave the other half clear to create a cool zone. If using gas, turn one of the burners to low. Lightly oil the grill grate.

On a lightly floured work surface, cut the dough into 4 equal pieces. Wrap 3 pieces in plastic wrap and set aside. Using your hands or a rolling pin, roll and stretch the remaining dough piece into a circle about 10 inches (25 cm) in diameter and ¼ inch (6 mm) thick. Carefully transfer the dough disk to a baking sheet lightly dusted with flour and cover with a piece of parchment paper. Roll and stretch the remaining pieces of dough in the same way, stacking them between sheets of parchment paper.

Brush one side of a dough disk with olive oil and place it, oiled side down, on the hot part of the grill. Repeat with a second dough disk if you have room on the grill. Grill just until slightly charred on the bottom and the crust has begun to puff and turn crispy, about 2 minutes. Using tongs and a wide spatula or pizza peel, flip the pizza and move it to the cool area of the grill. Top with ¾ cup (3 oz/90 g) cheese and a few tomato slices. Scatter some of the onion and olives over the tomatoes. Cover and grill until the bottom of the pizza is browned and crisped and the cheese has melted, 3–5 minutes. Transfer to a warm oven while grilling the remaining pizzas.

Carefully transfer the pizzas to a cutting board and top each with some of the arugula and basil. Drizzle with a little olive oil and sprinkle with salt. Cut into wedges and serve.

WINE SUGGESTION: A RICH, FRUITY RED, SUCH AS BARBERA D'ASTI OR BARBERA D'ALBA

Spaghetti alla carbonara is my son's favorite pasta. But he also loves pizza, so it was inevitable that one day the two would meet in this inspired mash-up. Serve this rich pizza with a simple arugula salad. Any extra white sauce is delicious on cooked pasta.

carbonara pizza with pancetta & egg

FOR THE WHITE SAUCE

3 tablespoons unsalted butter

1 shallot, minced, about ¼ cup (1½ oz/45 g)

3 tablespoons minced garlic

¼ cup (2 fl oz/60 ml) dry white wine

1½ cups (12 fl oz/375 ml) heavy cream

½ cup (2 oz/60 g) freshly grated *pecorino romano* cheese

Fine sea salt and freshly ground black pepper

¼ lb (125 g) pancetta, cut into cubes

Extra-virgin olive oil for greasing

2 recipes Pizza Dough (page 208)

1 lb (500 g) fresh mozzarella cheese, thinly sliced

¼ cup (1 oz/30 g) freshly grated *pecorino romano* cheese

Fine sea salt and freshly ground black pepper

2 large eggs

serves 6–8

To make the white sauce, in a heavy-bottomed saucepan, melt the butter over medium heat. Add the shallot and cook, stirring often, until slightly softened, about 5 minutes. Add the garlic and cook, stirring, until fragrant, 1–2 minutes; do not let it brown. Pour in the wine and raise the heat to medium-high. Let the wine bubble until almost evaporated. Stir in the cream and bring to a boil. Reduce the heat to medium and simmer gently until the sauce is thickened, 20–25 minutes. Stir in the cheese and season with ¼ teaspoon salt and a few grindings of pepper. Cook, stirring, until the cheese is melted, 2–3 minutes longer. Remove from the heat and cover.

If using a pizza stone or a baking steel, place it in the oven. Preheat the oven to 500°F (260°C).

Put the pancetta in a cold frying pan, preferably cast iron, and place over medium heat. Cook, stirring occasionally, until browned and beginning to crisp, 10–15 minutes. Transfer to a paper towel–lined plate.

Lightly oil two 13- or 14-inch (33- or 35-cm) round pizza pans or two 12-by-17-inch (30-by-43-cm) rimmed baking sheets. If baking the pizza directly on a stone or steel, you will need to assemble the pizzas one at a time on a lightly floured pizza peel. Using your hands or a rolling pin, roll and stretch out the pizza dough out toward the rim of the pan or peel. If the dough springs back, let it rest for a minute, then continue. Spread a thin layer of the white sauce on the dough, leaving a 1-inch (2.5-cm) border. Arrange the mozzarella on the sauce and scatter the pancetta on top. Sprinkle with the *pecorino romano* and season generously with pepper.

Bake one of the pizzas until the cheese is melted but not browned, about 5 minutes. Remove the pizza from the oven, crack 1 egg into the center, and season with salt and pepper. Bake until the egg is just set, about 3 minutes longer. Let cool while you repeat with the second pizza. Let it cool briefly, then cut the pizzas into wedges and serve.

WINE SUGGESTION: GAVI OR ANOTHER WHITE WITH ENOUGH ACIDITY TO COMPLEMENT THE SLIGHTLY RICH SAUCE

fish & meat

Herbs and herb sauces—think classic pesto—feature prominently in the cuisine of Liguria, a mountainous region dotted with picturesque seaside villages on Italy's northwestern coast. Here, a mix of herbs plus zesty lemon dresses up simple roasted swordfish. The sauce is also fantastic on pasta.

roasted swordfish with ligurian herb sauce

1 cup (1 oz/30 g) fresh flat-leaf parsley leaves

1 cup (1 oz/30 g) fresh basil leaves

3 tablespoons fresh marjoram leaves

3 cloves garlic, coarsely chopped

Finely grated zest of 1 lemon, plus 4 thin lemon slices

Fine sea salt and freshly ground black pepper

¼ cup (1 oz/30 g) finely chopped walnuts

¼ cup (1½ oz/45 g) finely chopped pitted black olives, such as Gaeta or Kalamata

3 tablespoons extra-virgin olive oil, plus more for drizzling

4 swordfish steaks, 6–8 oz (185–250 g) each and about ¾ inch (2 cm) thick

serves 4

Preheat the oven to 450°F (230°C).

On a cutting board, combine the parsley, basil, marjoram, and garlic. Using a sharp knife or a mezzaluna, chop them together finely. Add the lemon zest and 1 teaspoon salt and chop a few more times. Transfer the mixture to a bowl and stir in the walnuts, olives, and the 3 tablespoons olive oil to form a coarse, spoonable paste. Cover with a thin layer of olive oil and set aside.

Place the swordfish steaks in a shallow roasting pan. Drizzle about 1 tablespoon olive oil over them and rub it in gently. Season lightly with salt and pepper. Lay a lemon slice on each steak. Roast until the fish is cooked through, about 15 minutes.

Arrange the fish on a serving platter or on individual plates and spoon the herb sauce on top. Serve right away.

WINE SUGGESTION: VERMENTINO FROM SARDINIA OR TUSCANY, OR PIGATO FROM LIGURIA

Sea scallops have a sweet, nutty flavor that pairs perfectly with this classic piquant green sauce of parsley, capers, and anchovies. When buying scallops, look for those labeled "dry" or "dry-pack." They are usually fresher and have a better flavor and texture than "wet" scallops.

panfried scallops with salsa verde

2 cups (2 oz/60 g) lightly packed fresh flat-leaf parsley leaves

2 imported Italian or Spanish anchovy fillets

1 clove garlic, coarsely chopped

½ cup (1 oz/30 g) fresh bread crumbs

1 tablespoon capers, rinsed and drained

Fine sea salt and freshly ground black pepper

1 tablespoon red wine vinegar

½ cup (4 fl oz/125 ml) extra-virgin olive oil, plus 2 tablespoons

1 cup (5 oz/155 g) unbleached all-purpose flour

1 lb (500 g) sea scallops, small side muscles removed

serves 4

In a food processor, combine the parsley, anchovies, garlic, bread crumbs, capers, ½ teaspoon salt, and a generous grinding of pepper. Pulse briefly to combine. Sprinkle in the vinegar and pulse again. With the motor running, drizzle in the ½ cup (4 fl oz/125 ml) olive oil and process until smooth. Scrape the sauce into a bowl.

Put the flour in a shallow bowl. Pat the scallops dry with paper towels and dredge lightly in the flour, shaking off the excess. In a large frying pan, heat the 2 tablespoons olive oil over medium heat. Arrange the scallops in the pan and sprinkle with a little salt and pepper. Sauté until nicely browned on the bottom, 2–3 minutes. Turn carefully and sauté until browned on the second side and opaque almost all the way through but still tender, 2–3 minutes longer.

Using a wide spatula, gently transfer the scallops to a serving platter and spoon some of the salsa verde over them. Serve, passing additional sauce at the table.

WINE SUGGESTION: ORVIETO, A DRY, EVERYDAY WHITE FROM UMBRIA

This mussel stew is great to serve for casual gatherings: everyone digs in and gets a little messy. Classic Neapolitan versions call for nothing more than mussels, tomatoes, oil, garlic, and parsley. I like to add a splash of wine and colorful, zesty *gremolata*.

mussel stew with fennel gremolata

FOR THE *GREMOLATA*

½ cup (¾ oz/20 g) finely chopped fennel fronds

¼ cup (⅓ oz/10 g) finely chopped fresh flat-leaf parsley

2 cloves garlic, minced

Finely grated zest of 1 lemon and 1 orange

½ cup (4 fl oz/125 ml) extra-virgin olive oil, plus more for drizzling

½ red onion, thinly sliced

4 cloves garlic, minced

1 can (28 oz/875 g) diced tomatoes

1 small fresh hot chile, minced, or a generous pinch of red pepper flakes

¾ cup (6 fl oz/180 ml) dry white wine

4 lb (2 kg) mussels, scrubbed and debearded, if needed

4 slices Bruschetta (page 20) or toasted country bread

serves 4

To make the *gremolata,* in a bowl, stir together the fennel fronds, parsley, garlic, and lemon and orange zests. Set aside.

In a large, wide saucepan big enough to hold the mussels, heat the olive oil over medium-low heat. Add the onion and garlic and sauté until the onion is softened, about 7 minutes. Stir in the tomatoes and chile and raise the heat to medium. Cook for 5 minutes, just enough to allow the flavors to blend. Pour in the wine, raise the heat to high, and bring to a boil. Slide in the mussels, discarding any that do not close to the touch, and cover the pan. Cook at a lively simmer until the mussels have opened, 5–7 minutes. Discard any mussels that fail to open.

Place a slice of bruschetta in the bottom of each of 4 shallow bowls. Ladle the stew over the bread. Drizzle a little olive oil on top of each serving, sprinkle with the *gremolata,* and serve.

WINE SUGGESTION: A CRISP WHITE, SUCH AS VERMENTINO DI SARDEGNA

Branzino, also known as Mediterranean sea bass, is one of my favorite fish. It's low in fat, but has a lovely buttery flavor and silky texture. It is delicious simply roasted with lemon and herbs.

roasted branzino with herbed farro

1½ cups (10½ oz/330 g) *farro*, rinsed and drained

4 cups (32 fl oz/1 l) chicken broth, preferably homemade (page 209)

2 lemons

6 tablespoons (3 fl oz/ 90 ml) extra-virgin olive oil, plus more for greasing and drizzling

½ small red onion, finely chopped

¼ cup (⅓ oz/10 g) finely chopped fresh herbs, such as basil, mint, parsley, and thyme

Fine sea salt and freshly ground black pepper

4 whole branzino, about 1 lb (500 g) each, cleaned and gutted by the fishmonger

8 fresh flat-leaf parsley sprigs

serves 4

In a large saucepan over medium-high heat, combine the *farro* and broth and bring to a boil. Reduce the heat to maintain a gentle simmer, cover, and cook until the *farro* is tender but still pleasantly chewy, 25–30 minutes. Drain and set aside.

Preheat the oven to 450°F (230°C).

Zest the lemons and reserve the fruit. In a large frying pan, heat 2 tablespoons of the olive oil over medium heat. Add the onion, chopped herbs, and half of the lemon zest and sauté until the onion is softened. Add the drained *farro*, 1 teaspoon salt, and a generous grinding of pepper and stir to mix well. Reduce the heat to medium-low and cook until the *farro* is heated through, about 5 minutes. Stir in the remaining zest. Cover to keep warm and set aside.

Cut the reserved lemons into 20 thin slices. Season the cavity and both sides of each fish with salt and pepper. Lightly oil a large rimmed baking sheet. Arrange the fish on the pan. Put 2 lemon slices and a parsley sprig in each cavity. Lay 3 lemon slices along the top of each fish and finish with another parsley sprig. Drizzle each fish with 1 tablespoon olive oil.

Roast until sizzling and lightly golden on top, 10–15 minutes. The flesh should be flaky and white, but still moist. Spoon the *farro* onto a large platter and top with the roasted branzino. Drizzle with a little more olive oil and serve.

WINE SUGGESTION: A CRISP WHITE FROM SOUTHERN ITALY, SUCH AS FALANGHINA OR GRECO DI TUFO

Tagliata, Italian for "cut," usually refers to a sliced beef steak, but it's also a great way to tackle thick, over-sized tuna steaks. The seared slices are served here with a rich eggplant salad.

tuna tagliata with eggplant salad & oregano oil

½ cup (½ oz/15 g) lightly packed fresh oregano leaves, plus ½ teaspoon minced

¾ cup (6 fl oz/180 ml) extra-virgin olive oil

Fine sea salt and freshly ground black pepper

1 lb (500 g) young eggplant, peeled and cut into ½-inch (12-mm) dice

2 teaspoons red wine vinegar

½ teaspoon minced fresh mint

2 large tuna steaks, each about ¾ lb (375 g) and 1 inch (2.5 cm) thick

1 clove garlic, crushed flat but left whole

serves 4

Chop the ½ cup (½ oz/15 g) oregano coarsely and transfer to a bowl. Add ½ cup (4 fl oz/125 ml) of the olive oil and salt to taste and mix well. Set aside.

In a large frying pan, heat the remaining ¼ cup (2 fl oz/60 ml) olive oil over medium heat. Add the eggplant and ½ teaspoon salt and stir well. Reduce the heat to medium-low and cook, stirring occasionally, until the eggplant is just tender, about 10 minutes. Transfer to a bowl, add the vinegar, and toss to mix. Stir in the minced oregano and mint and set aside.

Brush the tuna steaks with some of the infused oregano oil and season with salt and pepper. Pour the remaining oil (about 1 tablespoon) into a large, heavy-bottomed frying pan over medium-high heat and add the garlic. Cook for about 1 minute, using a spatula to press the garlic into the oil. Discard the garlic before it browns.

Arrange the tuna steaks in the pan and raise the heat to high. Sear for 2 minutes, then turn and sear on the second side for 2 minutes longer. Transfer to a cutting board and carve against the grain into slices ½ inch (12 mm) thick. Carefully fan the tuna slices on a serving platter and mound the eggplant salad next to it. Drizzle a little oregano oil over the tuna and eggplant salad (you may not use it all) and serve.

WINE SUGGESTION: VERMENTINO DI SARDEGNA, A CRISP WHITE FROM SARDINIA

Sardines are plentiful in southern Italy, where you will find them marinated, fried, baked, and grilled. They are nutritious, sustainable, and delectable. Here, stuffed with tuna, seasoned with lemon, and served over arugula, they make an especially appetizing main dish.

tuna-stuffed grilled sardines

4 oz (125 g) wild or baby arugula

1 large fennel bulb, cored and cut crosswise into thin slices

3 tablespoons extra-virgin olive oil

8 large whole sardines, scales, guts, and backbones removed by the fishmonger

1 can (2.8 oz/85 g) imported Italian tuna in olive oil, drained but oil reserved

2 tablespoons minced fresh flat-leaf parsley

2 teaspoons capers, drained and finely chopped

Fine sea salt and freshly ground black pepper

Juice of 1 lemon

Lemon slices for serving

serves 4

Prepare a fire in a charcoal grill or preheat a gas grill to high.

In a bowl, toss the arugula and fennel with 2 tablespoons of the olive oil. Arrange the arugula and fennel on a serving platter.

Rinse the sardines inside and out and carefully pat them dry with paper towels. In a small bowl, combine the tuna, parsley, and capers. Spoon a little of the tuna mixture into the cavity of each sardine. Close the sardines around the filling and secure them with toothpicks. Brush them with a little of the reserved oil from the can and sprinkle with salt.

Arrange the sardines carefully on the grill grate and cook until charred and nicely grill marked on the bottom, 3–4 minutes. Using a spatula, gently turn the sardines and grill until charred on the second side and the flesh is opaque throughout, about 3 minutes longer.

Transfer the sardines to the bed of arugula and fennel and drizzle with the remaining 1 tablespoon olive oil. Sprinkle with the lemon juice and some pepper. Add the lemon slices to the platter and serve right away.

WINE SUGGESTION: A CRISP WHITE, SUCH AS VERDICCHIO

As a girl, I used to stick my hand into the wet sand at the edge of the Adriatic Sea and pull up *telline*—tiny, thin-shelled oval clams—split them open, and eat them on the spot. My kids love clams just as much, whether tossed with linguine or in this spicy Italian-style surf 'n' turf.

clams with white wine, tomatoes & sausage

1 lb (500 g) sweet or hot Italian sausages, each link cut crosswise into 4–6 pieces

¾ cup (6 fl oz/180 ml) dry white wine

2 tablespoons extra-virgin olive oil, plus more for drizzling

3 large cloves garlic, crushed flat but left whole

1¼ cups (9 oz/280 g) canned diced tomatoes

1 small fresh hot chile, minced, or a generous pinch of red pepper flakes

4 dozen small clams, such as Manila or littleneck (about 3 lb/1.5 kg), scrubbed

Fine sea salt

¼ cup (⅓ oz/10 g) coarsely chopped fresh flat-leaf parsley

4–6 slices Bruschetta (page 20)

serves 4–6

Put the sausages in a dry frying pan and pour in ½ cup (4 fl oz/125 ml) of the wine and ½ cup (4 fl oz/125 ml) water. Bring to a boil over medium-high heat, cover, and reduce the heat to medium. Simmer for 5 minutes. Using tongs, turn the sausages, then re-cover and simmer for 5 minutes longer. Uncover, raise the heat to medium-high, and cook, turning often, until the liquid has evaporated and the sausages are browned. Transfer to a bowl and set aside.

Add the olive oil and garlic to the pan and cook over medium heat until the garlic is fragrant and just beginning to sizzle, about 2 minutes (do not let it brown). Add the tomatoes and chile and cook, stirring occasionally, until the tomatoes have thickened, 15–20 minutes. Return the sausages to the pan and add the clams and the remaining ¼ cup (2 fl oz/60 ml) wine. Cover and raise the heat to medium-high. Cook at a lively simmer until the clams open, about 10 minutes. Taste and add salt, if needed. Stir in the parsley and remove from the heat.

Spoon the clams and sausages into shallow bowls, dividing evenly. Ladle the sauce over. Tuck a slice of bruschetta on the side of each bowl and serve.

WINE SUGGESTION: A CRISP WHITE, SUCH AS VERMENTINO DI SARDEGNA, OR A LIGHT-TO-MEDIUM RED, SUCH AS MONTEPULCIANO D'ABRUZZO

I grew up eating panfried breaded fish fillets, served simply with lemon wedges. Instead of using the classic (somewhat heavy) egg-crumb coating, I like to sauté the bread crumbs in the same pan as the fish, creating a loose, light, and crunchy topping.

sole fillets with hazelnut bread crumbs

¼ cup (1 oz/30 g) dried bread crumbs

¼ cup (1 oz/30 g) toasted and finely chopped hazelnuts (see Cook's Note, page 62)

1 large clove garlic, crushed in a garlic press

1 tablespoon minced fresh flat-leaf parsley

Fine sea salt

2 tablespoons unsalted butter

4 sole fillets, about 6 oz (185 g) each

2 tablespoons extra-virgin olive oil

1 lemon, cut into wedges

serves 4

In a small bowl, stir together the bread crumbs, hazelnuts, garlic, parsley, and ½ teaspoon salt.

In a large frying pan, melt the butter over medium heat. Stir in the bread-crumb mixture and sauté until the crumbs are crisped and golden, about 5 minutes. Reduce the heat to medium-low. Spread the bread-crumb mixture in an even layer in the pan and lay the fillets on top. Drizzle the olive oil over the fish and cook until the edges of the fillets are opaque, 3–4 minutes. Turn and cook until the flesh is opaque throughout, 3–4 minutes longer.

Using a wide spatula, carefully transfer the fish to a serving platter or to individual plates. Spoon the crumbs over the fish and serve with the lemon wedges.

WINE SUGGESTION: ARNEIS ROERO, A FLORAL WHITE FROM PIEDMONT

Just a few blocks away from my aunts' apartment in Rome was a small *rosticceria* that sold the juiciest rotisserie chickens I've ever had. Once in awhile we would pick up a chicken on the way home, along with a helping of fried potatoes and zucchini.

butterflied chicken roasted with lemons

¼ cup (2 fl oz/60 ml) extra-virgin olive oil

1 teaspoon fennel pollen or crushed fennel seed

1 organic free-range chicken, about 4 lb (2 kg)

1 lemon, halved

Coarse or fine sea salt and freshly ground black pepper

8 cloves garlic

serves 4

Preheat the oven to 450°F (230°C). In a small bowl, whisk together the olive oil and fennel pollen. Let stand at room temperature while you prepare the chicken.

Lay the chicken, breast side down, on a sturdy work surface with the drumsticks pointing toward you. Grip the chicken's tail (the pointy flap at the bottom). Using poultry shears or sharp kitchen shears, cut up along each side of the backbone, cutting all the way through. Remove the backbone and discard (or save for making stock). Turn the chicken over and push down on it between the breasts until the sternum breaks. Continue to push until the chicken is flattened, or butterflied.

Lay the chicken, skin side up, in a roasting pan that holds it snugly. Pour the fennel oil over the chicken and rub it all over the surface with your fingers. Squeeze 1 lemon half over the chicken and season with about 1 teaspoon salt and lots of pepper. Cut the remaining lemon half into small chunks and strew them around the chicken, along with the garlic, tucking a few pieces of one or the other into various nooks.

Roast the chicken for 20 minutes. Reduce the heat to 400°F (200°C) and roast until the chicken is beautifully browned and the juices run clear when you insert a fork into the thickest part of a thigh or an instant-read thermometer inserted into the thickest part of a thigh and breast away from the bone registers 165°F (74°C), about 40 minutes longer.

Tent with aluminum foil and let rest for 10 minutes. To serve, using clean poultry shears or a chef's knife, cut the chicken into 10 serving pieces (2 legs, 2 thighs, 2 wings, and each breast half cut in half). Transfer to a platter and spoon the pan juices, including the garlic and lemon pieces, over the chicken. Serve right away.

WINE SUGGESTION: AN EARTHY RED, SUCH AS NEGROAMARO FROM PUGLIA OR NERO D'AVOLA FROM SICILY

My mom often made simple, savory chicken in a skillet for supper, sometimes with a cut-up whole chicken, sometimes with just thighs, simmered to juicy tenderness. Here's my version, which features meaty olives and a surprise ingredient—mildly spicy jalapeño chile.

chicken thighs with green olives & lemon

1 tablespoon extra-virgin olive oil

8 skin-on, bone-in chicken thighs

Fine sea salt and freshly ground black pepper

1 large red onion, halved and thinly sliced

2 cloves garlic, thinly sliced

1 small jalapeño chile, seeded and minced

4 tablespoons (⅓ oz/10 g) chopped fresh flat-leaf parsley

½ cup (4 fl oz/125 ml) dry white wine

1 cup (4 oz/125 g) pitted meaty green olives, such as Cerignola, quartered

Zest and juice of 1 lemon, zest removed in thin strips

serves 4

In a large ovenproof frying pan, warm the olive oil over medium heat. Season the chicken thighs on both sides with salt and pepper. Arrange 4 of the thighs, skin side down, in the pan. Cook, without turning, until crispy and golden brown on the bottom, 5–6 minutes. Turn and cook until browned on the second side, 3–4 minutes longer. Transfer to a plate. Repeat to brown the remaining thighs. Pour off and discard all but about 2 tablespoons of the fat in the pan.

Reduce the heat to medium-low, add the onion to the pan, and sauté until beginning to wilt, 3–4 minutes. Add the garlic, jalapeño, and 2 tablespoons of the parsley and sauté until the onion is soft, about 4 minutes longer.

Return all of the chicken thighs, skin side up, to the pan and pour in ¼ cup (2 fl oz/60 ml) of the wine. Simmer gently, uncovered, until most of the wine has evaporated, about 10 minutes. Turn the chicken pieces and add the olives and lemon zest. Pour in the remaining ¼ cup wine and cook at a gentle simmer until most of the wine has evaporated, about 10 minutes longer. Add the lemon juice and raise the heat to medium. Turn the thighs and cook until opaque throughout and the juices run clear when you insert a fork into the thickest part of a thigh, about 5 minutes longer.

Position a broiler pan 4 inches (10 cm) below the heat source and preheat the broiler. Transfer the frying pan to the broiler and broil just to brown and crisp the chicken skin, 1–2 minutes.

Transfer the thighs to a serving platter and pour the pan juices over them. Sprinkle the remaining 2 tablespoons parsley on top and serve right away.

WINE SUGGESTION: PINOT GRIGIO FROM ALTO ADIGE

Rabbit is a fall staple in the mountainous regions of Italy, such as Abruzzo, where my family is from. With a texture that hovers somewhere between free-range chicken and turkey, rabbit is best roasted, with some pancetta thrown in for added succulence.

roasted rabbit with rosemary, sage & thyme

4 tablespoons (2 fl oz/60 ml) extra-virgin olive oil

3 large cloves garlic, crushed flat but left whole

4 oz (125 g) pancetta, cut into small dice

1 rabbit, 2½–3 lb (1.25–1.5 kg), skinned, cleaned, and cut up into 10 serving pieces by the butcher

Fine sea salt and freshly ground black pepper

1 fresh sage sprig

1 fresh rosemary sprig

4 fresh thyme sprigs

½ cup (4 fl oz/125 ml) dry white wine

serves 4

Preheat the oven to 375°F (190°C).

Measure 1 tablespoon of the olive oil into a large Dutch oven or flameproof roasting pan. Add the garlic and pancetta and place the pan over medium heat. Sauté until the pancetta begins to crisp and render its fat, about 8 minutes. Remove the pan from the heat and lay the pieces of rabbit in it. Sprinkle with ½ teaspoon salt and a generous grinding of pepper.

Remove the leaves from the herb sprigs and chop coarsely. Scatter the herbs over the meat and drizzle evenly with the remaining 3 tablespoons olive oil. Pour in the wine, then spoon some of the sautéed pancetta over the rabbit pieces. Roast for 45 minutes, using tongs to turn the pieces and basting with the pan juices every 15 minutes or so.

Raise the oven temperature to 450°F (230°C) and roast until the meat is beautifully browned and the juices run clear when you insert a fork into the thickest piece away from the bone, about 15 minutes longer. Transfer to a serving platter, spoon the pan juices on top, and serve.

WINE SUGGESTION: A FRUITY RED, SUCH AS DOLCETTO D'ALBA OR CHIANTI CLASSICO

I enjoy lean, quick-cooking pork tenderloin most in panfried dishes like this, which gets a boost from earthy porcini and the flavorful, slightly sweet Marsala wine.

pork scaloppine with marsala & porcini

1 oz (30 g) dried porcini mushrooms, steeped in 1 cup (8 fl oz/250 ml) boiling water for 30 minutes

1 tablespoon unsalted butter

1 tablespoon extra-virgin olive oil

1 clove garlic, crushed in a garlic press

Fine sea salt and freshly ground black pepper

1 teaspoon minced fresh rosemary, plus sprigs for garnish

1 pork tenderloin, 1–1½ lb (500–750 g), patted dry and cut crosswise into scaloppine 1 inch (2.5 cm) thick

1 small red onion, finely chopped

¼ cup (2 fl oz/60 ml) dry Marsala wine

½ cup (4 fl oz/125 ml) chicken broth, preferably homemade (page 209)

serves 4

Drain the mushrooms, reserving the liquid. Chop the mushrooms and set aside. Strain the mushroom broth into a clean bowl through a fine-mesh sieve lined with a damp paper towel. Set aside.

In a large frying pan, melt the butter with the olive oil over medium-low heat. In a small bowl, combine the garlic, 1 teaspoon salt, and the minced rosemary and mix into a paste. When the butter is melted and beginning to sizzle, add the garlic-rosemary paste to the pan and cook, stirring, until the garlic is fragrant, about 2 minutes. Arrange the scaloppine in the pan and raise the heat to medium-high. Grind a little pepper over the pork and cook, without turning, until lightly browned on the bottom, about 4 minutes. Turn and cook until browned on the second side, 3–4 minutes longer. Transfer to a warmed serving platter and tent loosely with aluminum foil to keep warm.

Add the onion to the pan and cook, stirring often, until it just begins to soften, 3–4 minutes. Raise the heat to high and stir in the wine. Let it bubble for about 1 minute, then pour in the reserved porcini broth and the chicken broth. Cook at a lively simmer until the liquid has reduced by about half, 3–5 minutes.

Spoon the sauce over the scaloppine, garnish with rosemary sprigs, and serve.

WINE SUGGESTION: BARBERA D'ASTI OR BARBERA D'ALBA, CLASSIC REDS FROM PIEDMONT

If you really want to hew to tradition—and create drama—you can pour the hot cooked polenta onto a slab or board right on the table and ladle the *ragù* over it, letting guests scoop up bites with slices of rustic bread. For the sake of practicality, I use a platter.

pork rib ragù with polenta

FOR THE PORK RIB *RAGÙ*

2 tablespoons vegetable oil

3 lb (1.5 kg) meaty pork spare ribs, cut into individual ribs

Fine sea salt and freshly ground black pepper

1 large carrot, peeled and finely chopped

1 yellow onion, finely chopped

1 rib celery, finely chopped

1 clove garlic, crushed flat but left whole

¾ cup (6 fl oz/180 ml) dry red wine

1 can (28 oz/875 g) diced tomatoes

1 bay leaf

FOR THE POLENTA

6–7 cups (48–56 fl oz/ 1.5–1.75 l) chicken broth, preferably homemade (page 209), or water

Fine sea salt (optional)

1½ cups (10½ oz/330 g) polenta

3 tablespoons unsalted butter, at room temperature

Freshly grated Parmigiano-Reggiano cheese for serving

serves 4–6

To make the *ragù*, warm the oil in a large, heavy-bottomed pot over medium heat. Add as many ribs as will fit without crowding the pot and season with salt and pepper. Brown the ribs on the first side, about 4 minutes. Using tongs, turn and brown on the second side, about 4 minutes longer. Transfer to a platter. Repeat to brown the remaining ribs.

Discard all but 2 tablespoons of the fat remaining in the pot. Add the carrot, onion, celery, and garlic to the fat in the pot and stir to coat. Reduce the heat to medium-low and sauté the vegetables until softened, about 7 minutes. Raise the heat to medium-high, pour in the wine, and stir to scrape up any browned bits from the pot bottom. Simmer for 1 minute, then add the tomatoes and bay leaf. Return the ribs to the pot along with any accumulated juices and bring to a boil. Reduce the heat to maintain a low simmer. Cover and cook very gently, stirring from time to time, until the meat is tender, about 2 hours. Uncover and cook until the sauce has thickened, about 1 hour longer. Remove and discard the garlic. Transfer the ribs to a clean platter and let cool briefly. Cut the meat off the bones, shred it with your fingers, and return the meat to the pot. Discard the bones.

To make the polenta, bring the broth to a boil in a heavy-bottomed saucepan over medium-high heat. If you are using water, stir in 1 teaspoon salt. Sprinkle in the polenta in a very slow, steady stream, stirring constantly to prevent lumps from forming. Reduce the heat to medium and cook, stirring often with a wooden spoon, until the polenta is very thick and comes away cleanly from the sides and bottom of the pan, about 30 minutes. Stir in the butter.

Divide the polenta among wide, shallow bowls and spoon the *ragù* over the top. Sprinkle each serving with some cheese and serve.

WINE SUGGESTION: MONICA DI SARDEGNA, AN EASY-DRINKING, EVERYDAY RED FROM SARDINIA

Porchetta—highly seasoned, deboned, stuffed, and roasted whole pig—is a marketplace staple in many parts of Italy. Here is my simplified home-cooked version, which has all the flavors of the original. Serve it as a main course or stuffed inside crusty rolls for lunch.

slow-cooked porchetta-style roast

3 tablespoons fennel seeds, toasted

3 tablespoons coarse sea salt

3 tablespoons peppercorns

1 boneless pork shoulder, about 3½ lb (1.75 kg), butterflied by the butcher to lay flat

4 tablespoons (2 fl oz/60 ml) extra-virgin olive oil

2 tablespoons minced garlic

2 tablespoons minced fresh rosemary, plus 1 or 2 sprigs for garnish

2 tablespoons minced fresh sage, plus 1 or 2 sprigs for garnish

2 tablespoons finely grated lemon zest

serves 8–10

In a spice grinder or a mini food processor, combine the fennel seeds, the salt, and the peppercorns and grind finely.

Lay the pork shoulder open on a cutting board. Drizzle 2 tablespoons of the olive oil over the pork and rub to coat the entire surface. Sprinkle half of the fennel mixture over the pork, then sprinkle the garlic, minced rosemary and sage, and lemon zest on top. Roll up the pork and tie securely with kitchen string at 1-inch (2.5-cm) intervals. Rub the remaining 2 tablespoons olive oil over the outside of the pork and sprinkle with the remaining fennel mixture.

Place the pork on a rack set inside a roasting pan. Refrigerate, uncovered, overnight. Let stand at room temperature for 1 hour. Preheat the oven to 275°F (135°C).

Roast the pork, uncovered, until the top is deeply browned, the meat is fork-tender throughout, and an instant-read thermometer inserted into the thickest part registers 160°–170°F (71°–77°C), about 3½ hours. Remove from the oven, tent with aluminum foil, and let rest for at least 15 minutes. Remove the kitchen string, slice the roast thinly or thickly, and transfer the slices to a serving platter. Spoon the pan juices on top and garnish with the rosemary and sage sprigs.

WINE SUGGESTION: A MEDIUM-BODIED RED SUCH AS DOLCETTO D'ALBA OR DOLCETTO DI DOGLIANI

When it comes to pork, I'll take mine with a little fat, please. Why eat pork that has been bred to be so lean that it is flavorless and cooks up tough as shoe leather? Good pork from heritage producers and small farms is increasingly available, so seek it out for these pan-seared chops.

pan-seared pork chops with meyer lemon

2 tablespoons extra-virgin olive oil

3 cloves garlic, very thinly sliced

4 fresh bay leaves, or 6 dried bay leaves

2 Meyer lemons, 1 thinly sliced and 1 halved

4 bone-in, center-cut pork chops, 6–8 oz (185–250 g) each

Fine sea salt and freshly ground black pepper

serves 4

In a large cast-iron or other heavy-bottomed frying pan, heat the olive oil, garlic, and bay leaves over medium-low heat. Sauté until the garlic is lightly golden and the oil is infused with the aroma of garlic and bay leaf, about 5 minutes. Transfer the garlic and bay leaves to a plate and set aside. Return the pan to the heat and add the lemon slices. Cook, turning once, until lightly browned, about 2 minutes per side. Transfer to the plate with the garlic and bay leaves.

Season the pork chops with salt and pepper. Arrange in the pan and raise the heat to medium-high. Sear until nicely browned on the bottom, 2–3 minutes. Turn the chops and cook until browned on the second side, 2–3 minutes longer. Squeeze the lemon halves over the chops and turn to coat them with the juice. Return the garlic, bay leaves, and lemon slices to the pan and reduce the heat to medium-low. Cook until the chops are cooked through, 3–4 minutes longer. The pork chop should spring back but still feel tender if gently pressed with a finger, and the center should be very slightly pink.

Transfer the pork chops to a serving platter and spoon the pan juices, along with the lemon slices, over the top. Serve right away.

WINE SUGGESTION: VALPOLICELLA RIPASSO, A ROBUST RED THAT HAS BEEN EXPOSED TO GRAPE SKINS USED TO MAKE AMARONE

Stuffed zucchini was a childhood favorite of mine and I still love it. If you buy your squash at the farmers' market, choose a variety of shapes and colors—it will make this dish quite striking. You'll likely have some stuffing left over. Use it to make meatballs or a small meatloaf.

meatball-stuffed summer squash

1 clove garlic, lightly crushed, plus 2 cloves garlic, chopped

1 can (28 oz/875 g) diced tomatoes, with juice

5–7 tablespoons (3–3.5 fl oz/ 80–110 ml) extra-virgin olive oil, plus more for greasing

Fine sea salt and freshly ground black pepper

12 mixed summer squash (long and round shapes and green and yellow), about 4½ lb (2 kg) total weight

½ lb (250 g) ground beef

1 cup (2 oz/60 g) fresh bread crumbs

½ cup (2 oz/60 g) freshly grated Parmigiano-Reggiano cheese

2 tablespoons minced fresh flat-leaf parsley

1 large egg, lightly beaten

2 tablespoons half-and-half

serves 6–8

Preheat the oven to 375°F (190°C).

In a bowl, combine the crushed garlic, tomatoes and juice, and 3 tablespoons of the olive oil. Season lightly with salt and stir to blend. Set aside.

Cut the ends off the long squash. Cut the top off the round squash and, if necessary, a sliver off the bottom so they stand upright. Using a corer, carefully hollow out a tunnel through the long squash. Using a melon baller or corer, carefully scoop out the inside of the round squash. Be careful not to cut all the way through. Set aside.

In a bowl, combine the ground beef, bread crumbs, cheese, chopped garlic, parsley, egg, half-and-half, 1 teaspoon salt, and a few grindings of pepper and mix thoroughly. Using your fingers or a small spoon, fill the squash cavities with the meat mixture; do not pack them too tightly as the filling will expand during roasting.

Lightly oil a large baking dish or 2 smaller dishes. Spoon a layer of the tomato mixture on the bottom of the prepared dish. Arrange the squash in the dish so they fit snugly. Spoon the remaining tomato mixture over the squash and drizzle the remaining 2–4 tablespoons olive oil on top. Cover with aluminum foil and roast until the squash is very tender and can be easily pierced with a fork, about 1½ hours. Let cool for at least 5 minutes before serving. Serve warm or at room temperature.

WINE SUGGESTION: A LIGHTER RED, SUCH AS BARDOLINO OR PINOT NERO

As teenagers, my sister and I would head into the hills of Abruzzo with our friends for dinner. The enticing aroma of meat cooking over a wood-burning fire would let us know when we were close. Traditional *arrosticini* have only lamb, olive oil, salt, and lemon, but I add garlic and rosemary.

abruzzese-style lamb skewers

Long (about 12-inch/30-cm) wooden skewers, soaked in water for 30 minutes

2 lb (1 kg) boneless leg of lamb with some marbling of fat, cut into precise ¾-inch (2-cm) cubes

¼ cup (2 fl oz/60 ml) extra-virgin olive oil

Fine sea salt

3 cloves garlic, very thinly sliced

1 large fresh rosemary sprig, cut into 2-inch (5-cm) pieces, plus additional sprigs for garnish

1 lemon, cut into wedges

serves 4–6

Drain the skewers. Divide the lamb cubes among the skewers, threading them tightly so they are touching and leaving a length of skewer empty at one end to use as a handle. Arrange the assembled skewers in a single layer on a rimmed baking sheet or in a large, shallow baking dish. Drizzle the olive oil over the skewers and rub with your fingers to make sure all of the meat is well coated. Sprinkle the meat lightly with salt and scatter the garlic and rosemary pieces on top. Let stand at room temperature for 20–30 minutes.

Prepare a fire in a charcoal grill or preheat a gas grill to high. Place the skewers on the grill grate directly over the heat and sear until browned on the first side, about 3 minutes. Turn and sear until browned on the second side, about 2 minutes longer. The interior of the meat should still be slightly pink. Using tongs, transfer the skewers to a large serving platter. Garnish the platter with the rosemary sprigs and lemon wedges and serve.

WINE SUGGESTION: NERO D'AVOLA, THE ROBUST RED FROM SICILY

Lamb is popular in the mountains of Abruzzo, where it is served roasted, in stews, and, of course, from the grill. The herb and almond pesto, I confess, is my embellishment. The bright green, tangy sauce beautifully complements the rich flavor of the seared chops.

grilled lamb chops with herb-almond pesto

FOR THE PESTO

1½ cups (1½ oz/45 g) lightly packed fresh basil leaves

1 cup (1 oz/30 g) lightly packed fresh flat-leaf parsley leaves

½ cup (½ oz/15 g) lightly packed fresh mint leaves

3 tablespoons slivered almonds, lightly toasted

2 cloves garlic, chopped

Fine sea salt

¾ cup (6 fl oz/180 ml) extra-virgin olive oil

2 teaspoons red or white balsamic vinegar

8 lamb chops, each about 1 inch (2.5 cm) thick

2 tablespoons extra-virgin olive oil

Fine sea salt and freshly ground black pepper

serves 4

Prepare a fire in a charcoal grill or preheat a gas grill to high.

To make the pesto, in a food processor, combine the basil, parsley, mint, almonds, garlic, and 1 teaspoon salt and process until coarsely chopped. Stop to scrape down the sides of the bowl as needed. With the motor running, drizzle in the olive oil and purée to a thick consistency. Scrape the pesto into a bowl and stir in the vinegar. Set aside.

Rub the lamb chops on all sides with the 2 tablespoons olive oil and season with salt and pepper. Arrange on the grill grate and grill over medium-high to high heat until seared and nicely grill marked on the first side, about 3 minutes. Turn and grill on the second side for about 3 minutes longer for medium-rare. Transfer to a platter, tent with aluminum foil, and let rest for 5 minutes.

Arrange 2 chops on each of 4 dinner plates, spoon a generous dollop of pesto on the side, and serve.

WINE SUGGESTION: NERO D'AVOLA, A STURDY SICILIAN RED, OR, AS A SPLURGE, BAROLO FROM PIEDMONT

A couple of years ago, I took a trip with my family to the Garfagnana area of Tuscany. We especially enjoyed the hearty cuisine in this corner of Italy. For lunch one day we shared a grilled *tagliata*—a sliced steak served with barely sautéed baby artichokes. It was so good I had to reproduce it in my kitchen.

sliced steak with garlic-sautéed artichokes

FOR THE SAUTÉED ARTICHOKES

Juice of 1 lemon

1 lb (500 g) fresh baby artichokes

¼ cup (2 fl oz/60 ml) extra-virgin olive oil

2 large cloves garlic, very thinly sliced

1 small fresh rosemary sprig

1 tablespoon minced fresh flat-leaf parsley

Fine sea salt and freshly ground black pepper

1 large boneless sirloin steak, about 1½ lb (750 g)

2 tablespoons extra-virgin olive oil

Fine sea salt and freshly ground black pepper

Juice of ½ lemon (optional)

serves 4

To make the artichokes, fill a bowl with cold water and add half of the lemon juice. Trim the ends of the artichokes and remove the tough outer leaves. Slice the tips off the inner leaves and quarter the artichokes. Remove any fuzzy choke, if present, and immerse the artichoke quarters in the lemon water.

In a large frying pan over medium-low heat, combine the olive oil, garlic, and rosemary and sauté just until the garlic begins to soften, about 5 minutes. Drain the artichokes and add to the pan. Add the parsley, 1 teaspoon salt, and a grinding of pepper and cook, stirring occasionally, until the artichokes are tender, 7–8 minutes. Sprinkle in the remaining lemon juice and cook for 1 minute longer. Cover to keep warm and set aside.

Prepare a fire in a charcoal grill or preheat a gas grill to medium-high. If using charcoal, spread the hot coals across one half of the bottom of the grill and leave the other half clear. Rub the steak with the 2 tablespoons olive oil. Sprinkle on both sides with salt and pepper. Put the steak on the grill directly over the heat and sear for 2 minutes. Turn and sear for 2 minutes on the second side. If using charcoal, move the steaks to indirect heat. If using gas, reduce the heat to medium. Grill for about 8 minutes longer for medium-rare, turning once or twice. Transfer to a cutting board, tent with aluminum foil, and let rest for 5 minutes.

Carve the steak against the grain into slices ½ inch (12 mm) thick and transfer to a platter. Spoon the artichokes around the steak and drizzle the pan juices over all. Squeeze the lemon half over the steaks if desired and serve.

WINE SUGGESTION: CHIANTI CLASSICO, THE DRY SANGIOVESE-BASED RED FROM TUSCANY

A true *Florentine bistecca*—an enormous piece of beef that comes from the region's famed Chianina cattle—is a marvel. While we may not have the exact same type of beef here, we can use wonderful, pasture-raised beef that grills beautifully to re-create this signature dish.

tuscan-style steak
with crispy potatoes

1½ lb (750 g) baby waxy-skinned potatoes, such as Yukon gold, scrubbed but skins left on, halved

4 tablespoons (2 fl oz/60 ml) extra-virgin olive oil

Fine sea salt and freshly ground black pepper

2 teaspoons red wine vinegar

1 teaspoon fresh lemon juice

1 teaspoon minced fresh hot chile or a generous pinch of dried red pepper flakes

3 small fresh rosemary sprigs

2 bone-in Porterhouse steaks, about 1 lb (500 g) each

serves 4

Put the potatoes in a large saucepan and add water to cover by 1 inch (2.5 cm). Bring to a boil over high heat, then reduce the heat to medium-high and cook until the potatoes are almost tender, about 10 minutes. Drain and set aside.

In a large frying pan over medium heat, warm 2 tablespoons of the olive oil. When the oil is shimmering, add the potatoes and toss gently to coat with the oil. Cook without turning until nicely browned on the bottom, about 5 minutes. Sprinkle with ½ teaspoon salt and pepper to taste, turn, and cook, again without turning, until browned on the second side, 5 minutes longer. Stir and cook for a few more minutes to finish browning the potatoes and crisping the edges.

Meanwhile, prepare a fire in a charcoal grill or preheat a gas grill to high. In a bowl, whisk together the remaining 2 tablespoons olive oil, the vinegar, lemon juice, and chile. If using charcoal, spread the hot coals across one half of the bottom of the grill and leave the other half clear to create a cool zone.

Tie the rosemary sprigs together at one end, using kitchen string, to make a brush. Using the rosemary, brush the marinade all over the steaks on both sides. Sprinkle on both sides with salt. Arrange the steaks on the grill directly over the heat and sear for 2 minutes. Turn and sear for 2 minutes on the second side. If using charcoal, move the steaks to indirect heat. If using gas, reduce the heat to medium and grill for about 8 minutes longer for medium-rare, turning once or twice and brushing again with the marinade as they cook. Transfer to a cutting board, tent with aluminum foil, and let rest for 5 minutes.

Divide each steak into 2 pieces (you will have to flip or fight for who gets the bones!) and arrange on 4 dinner plates. Spoon some potatoes around the steak and serve.

WINE SUGGESTION: REDS SUCH AS CHIANTI CLASSICO RISERVA OR A SANGIOVESE-BASED "SUPER-TUSCAN"

sides

Fragrant fennel, golden honey, and crushed pistachios give these colorful carrots a decidedly Mediterranean twist. Purple, gold, and red rainbow carrots make for a beautiful presentation, but if you can't find them, use regular orange ones.

roasted carrots with fennel, pistachios & honey vinaigrette

2 teaspoons fennel seeds, toasted and coarsely ground

3 tablespoons extra-virgin olive oil

1 lb (500 g) rainbow carrots, trimmed

Fine sea salt and freshly ground black pepper

1 tablespoon honey

2 teaspoons white balsamic vinegar

1 tablespoon crushed unsalted roasted pistachios

serves 4

Place the ground fennel seeds in a bowl and stir in the olive oil. Let steep for 30 minutes.

Preheat the oven to 400°F (200°C). Place the carrots on a rimmed baking sheet and drizzle the fennel-infused oil over them. Season lightly with salt and pepper. Roll the carrots around to coat completely with the oil, then arrange in a single layer. Roast until the carrots are tender and lightly browned, 20–25 minutes.

In a small bowl, whisk together the honey and vinegar. Drizzle over the carrots and turn to coat them. Sprinkle the pistachios on top and roast until the carrots are nicely caramelized, about 5 minutes longer. Serve warm.

WINE SUGGESTION: MONTEPULCIANO D'ABRUZZO, A FRUITY, MEDIUM-BODIED RED

In Calabria and other parts of southern Italy, hot peppers are enjoyed fresh or dried, ground into powder, and made into an ultra-spicy condiment used to flavor everything from pasta to grilled meat. Here, mild-tasting cauliflower is punched up with the chile spread, along with Meyer lemon, sweet currants, and toasty pine nuts.

cauliflower roasted with chile, meyer lemon, currants & pine nuts

1½–2 lb (750 g–1 kg) cauliflower (1 large head)

3 tablespoons extra-virgin olive oil

1 tablespoon hot Calabrian chile spread (available in Italian and specialty-food shops and online)

1 small Meyer lemon, quartered and cut crosswise into thin wedges

Fine sea salt

1½ tablespoons currants

2 tablespoons pine nuts, lightly toasted

serves 4–6

Preheat the oven to 450°F (230°C).

Separate the cauliflower into florets and cut the tender stem into bite-sized pieces, discarding any tough parts.

In a bowl, combine the cauliflower, olive oil, chile spread, lemon, and ½ teaspoon salt and toss to coat. Spread in a single layer on a rimmed baking sheet and roast for 10 minutes. Toss and roast until the cauliflower is tender and browned in spots, 5–10 minutes longer. Remove from the oven, sprinkle the currants on top, and toss gently to combine.

Transfer the cauliflower to a serving platter and sprinkle the pine nuts on top. Serve hot or warm.

WINE SUGGESTION: SICILIAN WHITES SUCH AS DRY AND FLINTY ETNA BIANCO OR CRISP GRILLO

To me, the smell of peppers frying calls up both Italian home kitchens and the small trattorie on city side streets. Serve these peppers as a side dish, stir them into a frittata, or toss with pasta. The zucchini flowers add subtle flavor and an extra splash of color.

sautéed mixed peppers with basil & balsamic

1¼–1½ lb (625–750 g) mixed peppers and chiles, preferably including red, yellow, and purple bell peppers and 1 or 2 mild chiles, such as poblano

3 tablespoons extra-virgin olive oil

2 cloves garlic, very thinly sliced

1 large red onion, cut into 8 wedges

3 small fresh thyme sprigs

Fine sea salt

12 zucchini flowers, cut crosswise into thin slices (optional)

1 tablespoon balsamic vinegar

2 tablespoons finely shredded fresh basil

serves 4

Seed the peppers and chiles and cut them into ½-inch (12-mm) strips.

In a large frying pan, heat the olive oil and garlic over medium-low heat. Sauté the garlic until softened but not browned, about 5 minutes. Add the peppers and onion and stir to coat with the oil. Raise the heat to medium and cook, stirring occasionally, until the peppers begin to soften, 5–7 minutes.

Stir in the thyme sprigs and ¼ teaspoon salt and cook until the peppers and onion are tender and browned in spots but not mushy, 20–25 minutes longer. Add the zucchini flowers, if using, and sauté until wilted but still brightly colored, about 2 minutes. Sprinkle in the vinegar and cook for another minute or two. Remove from the heat and stir in the shredded basil. Remove the thyme sprigs and serve.

WINE SUGGESTION: GRILLO, A PLEASANTLY ACIDIC WHITE FROM SICILY, OR A VERMENTINO FROM SARDINIA, SUCH AS VERMENTINO DI GALLURA

My great-uncle Eliseo was a diminutive man with a big personality and a talent for cooking. He made the best roast lamb with rosemary and cipollini onions every Easter. I've borrowed the flavors of his recipe but made the onions the star of the show.

balsamic-braised cippolini

2 lb (1 kg) cipollini onions

3 tablespoons unsalted butter

⅓ cup (3 fl oz/80 ml) chicken broth, preferably homemade (page 209)

⅓ cup (3 fl oz/80 ml) aged balsamic vinegar

2 small fresh thyme sprigs

1 small fresh rosemary sprig

Fine sea salt and freshly ground black pepper

⅓ cup (3 fl oz/80 ml) heavy cream

serves 6–8

Bring a large pot of water to a boil over high heat. Using a sharp paring knife, cut a small X into the root end of each onion. Gently drop the onions, skins and all, into the boiling water and blanch for 2 minutes. Drain immediately in a colander and let stand until cool enough to handle. When cooled, slip off the skins by pinching with your fingers. They should come off easily. Use the paring knife to assist you, if needed.

In a heavy-bottomed saucepan or frying pan large enough to hold all the onions snugly in a single layer, melt the butter over medium heat. When the butter has melted and begins to sizzle, raise the heat to medium-high and add the onions, stirring to coat. Cook until nicely browned on all sides, turning a few times as needed, about 5 minutes total. Reduce the heat to medium-low and pour in the broth and vinegar. Tuck in the thyme sprigs and the rosemary sprig. Sprinkle with ½ teaspoon salt and pepper to taste and gently stir to mix.

Cover and cook at a gentle simmer until the onions are just tender, 10–12 minutes. Uncover and raise the heat to medium-high. Stir in the cream and simmer until the sauce has thickened and reduced to a syrupy consistency.

Transfer the onions to a serving bowl, pour the sauce over the top, and serve.

WINE SUGGESTION: BARDOLINO, A LIGHT, FRUITY RED FROM THE VENETO

In Italy, winter squash is loved in simple sautés, roasted with herbs, or in soups and risottos. My favorite is delicata squash, with its cream-colored, green-striped edible skins and beautiful, sweet golden flesh that turns even sweeter in a hot oven.

roasted delicata squash with sage

2 tablespoons finely chopped fresh sage, plus 1 or 2 sprigs for garnish

¼ cup (2 fl oz/60 ml) extra-virgin olive oil

1 or 2 delicata squash, about 1½ lb (680 g)

Coarse sea salt and freshly ground black pepper

serves 4

Preheat the oven to 400°F (200°C).

In a small bowl, stir together the chopped sage and olive oil and let steep while you prepare the squash.

Cut the squash in half lengthwise and scoop out the seeds. Cut each half into 4 equal pieces. Place the squash on a rimmed baking sheet and drizzle the sage oil over all. Using your fingers, spread and rub the oil to coat the squash thoroughly. Season with salt and pepper.

Roast the squash, uncovered, until tender and browned in spots, 45–55 minutes. Transfer to a serving platter, garnish with the sage sprigs, and serve.

WINE SUGGESTION: VALPOLICELLA RIPASSO, A ROBUST RED THAT HAS BEEN EXPOSED TO GRAPE SKINS USED TO MAKE AMARONE

Eggplant was once a stand-in for meat in humble Italian homes. Now the vegetable is beloved in its own right for its silky texture and ability to absorb flavor. Here, the eggplant is roasted and then paired with equally lustrous mushrooms braised in white wine.

roasted eggplant with wine-braised mushrooms & citrus gremolata

3 long eggplants, such as Asian eggplants, about 1 lb (500 g) total weight

Fine sea salt and freshly ground black pepper

6 tablespoons (3 fl oz/90 ml) extra-virgin olive oil

2 shallots, finely diced, about ½ cup (3 oz/90 g)

1 lb (500 g) mixed mushrooms, such as cremini, portobello, and shiitake, brushed clean and sliced

3 or 4 fresh thyme sprigs

¾ cup (6 fl oz/180 ml) dry white wine

FOR THE CITRUS *GREMOLATA*

1 cup (1 oz/30 g) fresh flat-leaf parsley leaves

1 teaspoon fresh thyme leaves

1 large clove garlic, coarsely chopped

3 strips lemon zest

1 strip orange zest

serves 6–8

Cut the eggplants in half lengthwise. Make a series of deep crisscross slashes on the cut sides and sprinkle ½ teaspoon salt over them. Place, cut side down, on a wire rack or plate and let stand for 30–60 minutes.

Preheat the oven to 400°F (200°C). Line a baking sheet with parchment paper. Gently squeeze the eggplant halves to discard any bitter juices and pat dry. Brush 3 tablespoons of the olive oil on the cut sides, getting some inside the grooves. Place, cut side down, on the prepared baking sheet. Roast until the eggplants are very soft and their skins have turned brown, 30–40 minutes. Remove from the oven and tent with aluminum foil.

Meanwhile, in a large frying pan, heat the remaining 3 tablespoons olive oil over medium-low heat. Add the shallots and cook, stirring occasionally, until starting to soften, 5–7 minutes. Add the mushrooms and stir to coat them with the oil. Season with ½ teaspoon salt and a few grindings of pepper, and add the thyme sprigs. Raise the heat to medium and cook, stirring often, until the mushrooms have given off some liquid, about 10 minutes. Raise the heat to medium-high and pour in the wine. Let it bubble for 1–2 minutes, then reduce the heat to medium-low, and cook at a gentle simmer until the mushrooms are tender and the liquid is thickened but not completely evaporated, about 10 minutes longer.

To make the *gremolata*, mound the parsley, thyme, garlic, lemon zest, and orange zest on a cutting board and chop until finely minced.

Arrange the eggplant halves, cut side up, on a warmed serving platter and spoon the mushrooms over and around them. Spoon the pan juices over the vegetables, sprinkle the *gremolata* on top, and serve.

WINE SUGGESTION: DOLCETTO D'ALBA, A DRY RED FROM PIEDMONT WITH A SMOKY FINISH

Two of my favorite squashes, buttercup and kabocha, are now widely available. Their flesh is dense, golden, and sweet, and either is equally dazzling in this savory onion tart.

winter squash crostata with young pecorino

1 buttercup or kabocha squash, about 2 lb (1 kg)

4 tablespoons extra-virgin olive oil

1 red onion, finely chopped

1 teaspoon minced fresh thyme

2 large eggs

1 cup (8 fl oz/250 ml) heavy cream

Fine sea salt and freshly ground black pepper

Pastry Dough (page 40)

½ cup (2 oz/60 g) shredded *pecorino fresco* or other mild, semifirm sheep's milk cheese

½ cup (2 oz/60 g) freshly grated Parmigiano-Reggiano cheese

serves 6–8

Preheat the oven to 425°F (220°C). Cut the squash in half lengthwise and scoop out the seeds. Rub 1 tablespoon of the olive oil over the flesh and place the halves, cut side down, on a baking sheet. Bake until the skin is browned and the flesh is soft, about 40 minutes. Remove from the oven and let cool for 15 minutes. Scoop the flesh into a bowl and mash until smooth. Leave the oven on.

While the squash is baking, in a frying pan, heat the remaining 3 tablespoons olive oil over medium-low heat. Add the onion and thyme and sauté until the onion is softened, 7–8 minutes. Reduce the heat to low and cook, stirring from time to time, until the onion is very soft, about 30 minutes. In a large bowl, whisk together the eggs, cream, ¾ teaspoon salt, and a grinding of pepper. Add the mashed squash to the bowl and stir until the mixture is smooth.

On a lightly floured work surface, roll the dough out into an 11-inch (28-cm) circle. Press the dough into a 9-inch (23-cm) tart pan with removable sides. Trim the overhanging dough flush with the top of the pan sides; place the pan on a baking sheet. Spoon the onion into the crust and sprinkle the cheeses over it. Pour the squash-egg mixture over the cheese. Bake for 10 minutes. Reduce the oven temperature to 400°F (200°C) and bake until the filling is puffed up and set, about 20 minutes longer.

Transfer to a wire rack and let cool for 10 minutes. Remove the sides from the pan and transfer the *crostata* to a serving dish. Serve warm or at room temperature.

WINE SUGGESTION: BARBERA D'ALBA OR BARBERA D'ASTI, SPICY REDS FROM PIEDMONT

Beets are often seen in recipes from northern Italy—stirred into risotto, puréed and blended into pasta dough, or baked, as in this luscious scarlet gratin enriched with fontina cheese and walnuts. This is a winter favorite in our house.

beet gratin with fontina & walnuts

Butter for greasing

6 beets, peeled and thinly sliced with a knife or mandoline

2–3 tablespoons extra-virgin olive oil

6 oz (185 g) imported Italian fontina cheese, shredded

2 teaspoons minced fresh thyme

Fine sea salt and freshly ground black pepper

3 tablespoons heavy cream

3 tablespoons coarsely chopped walnuts

serves 6

Preheat the oven to 375°F (190°C). Butter an 8-inch (20-cm) square baking dish.

In a large bowl, combine the beets and olive oil and toss gently to coat. In a small bowl, stir together the cheese and thyme. Arrange about one-fourth of the beets in the bottom of the prepared dish, overlapping them very slightly. Sprinkle about one-fourth of the cheese and thyme mixture over the beets and season lightly with salt and pepper. Repeat to make 3 more layers, sprinkling the last layer of the herbed cheese with a little more salt and pepper. Drizzle the cream over the surface and sprinkle the walnuts on top.

Bake until the beets are tender and the walnuts are nicely browned, about 45 minutes. Remove the gratin from the oven and let rest for 5 minutes before serving.

WINE SUGGESTION: PINOT NERO, A LIGHT RED FROM ALTO ADIGE

My aunt Gilda loved summer squash and featured it in all sorts of simple preparations similar to this—an alternative to eggplant parmigiana. On hot summer days, serve it at room temperature, like my Zia Gilda did.

grilled summer squash parmesan

4 tablespoons (2 fl oz/60 ml) extra-virgin olive oil, plus more for greasing

2 cloves garlic, crushed flat but left whole

1 can (28 oz/875 g) diced or crushed tomatoes

Fine sea salt and freshly ground black pepper

10 fresh basil leaves, torn into small pieces

2 lb (1 kg) yellow summer squash, trimmed and cut lengthwise into slices 1/3 inch (9 mm) thick

12 oz (340 g) fresh mozzarella cheese, thinly sliced

1/4 cup (1 oz/30 g) freshly grated Parmigiano-Reggiano cheese

serves 4

In a saucepan over medium-low heat, warm 1 tablespoon of the olive oil. Add the garlic and sauté until fragrant, about 2 minutes. Add the tomatoes and 1/2 teaspoon salt, raise the heat to medium-high, and simmer, stirring occasionally, until the sauce has thickened, 25–30 minutes. Remove from the heat, remove and discard the garlic, and stir in about half of the basil. Set aside.

Prepare a fire in a charcoal grill or preheat a gas grill to medium-high. Preheat the oven to 375°F (190°C).

Put the squash on a baking sheet, drizzle with the remaining 3 tablespoons olive oil, season with salt and pepper, and toss to coat. Grill the squash, turning once, until lightly charred on both sides, 3–4 minutes per side. Transfer to a plate.

Lightly oil a large, shallow baking dish and spread about 1/4 cup (2 fl oz/60 ml) of the tomato sauce on the bottom. Arrange one-fourth of the squash in the dish. Top with one-third of the mozzarella slices and a few pieces of basil. Cover with another 1/4 cup sauce. Make 2 more layers of squash, mozzarella, basil, and sauce. Top with a final layer of squash and sauce and sprinkle with the Parmigiano. Bake, uncovered, until the juices are bubbling and the top is browned, about 35 minutes. Serve warm or at room temperature.

WINE SUGGESTION: A LIGHT-TO-MEDIUM RED, SUCH AS VALPOLICELLA SUPERIORE, BARDOLINO, OR MONTEPULCIANO D'ABRUZZO

Escarole, a delightfully savory member of the chicory family, is bitter and even a little tough when raw, but turns mellow, nutty, and tender when cooked. This ultra-flaky tart is impressive as a side dish or could be served as a light main course accompanied by cheeses and salumi.

escarole & olive tart

FOR THE TART DOUGH

2½ cups (12½ oz/390 g) unbleached all-purpose flour, plus more for dusting

¼ teaspoon fine sea salt

½ cup (4 oz/125 g) cold unsalted butter, cut into ½-inch (12-mm) dice

2 large eggs, lightly beaten

4–5 tablespoons (2–3 fl oz/60–80 ml) fresh lemon juice

Preheat the oven to 400°F (200°C).

To make the dough, in a food processor, combine the flour and salt and pulse to mix. Scatter the butter around the bowl and process until the mixture resembles coarse crumbs. Add the eggs and 4 tablespoons lemon juice and pulse just until the dough comes together. If the dough seems dry, add an additional tablespoon lemon juice and pulse until the dough comes together. Turn the dough out onto a lightly floured work surface and gently pat it into a disk. Wrap tightly in plastic wrap and refrigerate until ready to use.

To make the filling, in a large frying pan, heat the olive oil over medium-low heat. Add the onion and garlic and sauté until the onion is soft and translucent, 7–8 minutes. Add as much of the escarole and spinach to the pan as will fit without spilling. Raise the heat to medium, cover, and cook until wilted, about 1 minute, then add the rest of the greens to the pan and turn to coat with the oil. Add the olives, cayenne, and ¼ teaspoon salt and cook, stirring from time to time, until the greens are tender, 5–7 minutes. Stir in the lemon juice and cook for 2 minutes longer. Remove from the heat and let cool to room temperature.

FOR THE FILLING

3 tablespoons extra-virgin olive oil

1 yellow onion, finely chopped

3 cloves garlic, minced

1 lb (500 g) escarole, thinly sliced crosswise

1 lb (500 g) spinach

1 cup (5 oz/155 g) coarsely chopped pitted Gaeta or Kalamata olives

¼ teaspoon cayenne pepper

Fine sea salt

2 tablespoons fresh lemon juice

½ cup (2 oz/60 g) shredded *pecorino romano* cheese

1 large egg yolk, lightly beaten with 1 tablespoon water

serves 8

Remove the dough from the refrigerator and cut into 2 pieces, one slightly larger than the other. On a lightly floured work surface, roll the larger piece into a thin disk about 16 inches (40 cm) in diameter. Transfer the dough to a large (10–12-inch/25–30-cm) round cake pan, gently pressing it into the bottom and up the sides of the pan.

Spoon the filling into the crust and smooth the top. Sprinkle the cheese on top. Roll the second dough piece into a thin disk 11–13 inches (28–33 cm) in diameter. Carefully center it over the tart and pinch the edges gently to seal. Roll the overhanging crust in toward the pan edges to create a pretty rim. Brush with the egg mixture. Using a sharp paring knife, make 3 large slits in the top crust.

Bake until the crust is golden brown, 35–40 minutes. Transfer to a wire rack and let cool for about 15 minutes. To unmold, cover the tart with a large plate, carefully invert, and remove the pan, then invert again onto a serving plate. Cut into wedges and serve warm or at room temperature.

WINE SUGGESTION: A CRISP, DRY WHITE FROM SICILY, SUCH AS INZOLIA

Lacinato kale, also known as *cavolo nero* or dinosaur kale, has slender, blue-green crimped leaves and a mild cabbagelike taste and is one of fall's most alluring vegetables. Finely shredded, it is delicious raw in salads. Here, it is sautéed with chickpeas to make a hearty side dish.

spicy sautéed kale & chickpeas

3 large cloves garlic, very thinly sliced

¼ cup (2 fl oz/60 ml) extra-virgin olive oil

1 lb (500 g) lacinato (dinosaur) kale, tough bottom stems removed, leaves and tender stems coarsely shredded

1 can (14 oz/440 g) chickpeas, rinsed and drained

1 small fresh hot chile, seeded and minced, or a generous pinch of dried red pepper flakes

Fine sea salt

serves 4

In a large frying pan over medium-low heat, warm the garlic in the olive oil, stirring often, until softened but not browned, about 7 minutes. Put about half of the kale in the pan, or as much as will fit without spilling. Cover and let wilt for about 2 minutes, then uncover and add the rest of the kale. Using tongs, turn the greens to coat with the oil and garlic. Cover the pan and cook until the kale is tender, 15–20 minutes.

Uncover and stir in the chickpeas, chile, and 1 teaspoon salt. Raise the heat to medium and sauté until the chickpeas are heated through, about 5 minutes. Serve right away.

WINE SUGGESTION: PRIMITIVO, A SPICY RED FROM PUGLIA

Romano beans are no ordinary green bean. More flat than round, they have a meaty texture and earthy flavor. In my house, a bowl of these long-simmered beans often appears on the summer dinner table alongside roast chicken, sautéed chicken cutlets, or grilled fish.

tomato-braised romano beans with basil

2 tablespoons extra-virgin olive oil

2 cloves garlic, crushed flat but left whole

1 lb (500 g) romano beans (flat green beans), stem ends removed, cut in half crosswise

2 cups (14 oz/440 g) canned diced tomatoes

1 small fresh hot chile, seeded and minced, or a generous pinch of red pepper flakes

Fine sea salt

2 tablespoons coarsely chopped fresh basil

serves 4

In a large frying pan over medium-low heat, combine the olive oil and garlic and heat until the garlic begins to sizzle, about 3 minutes. Press on the garlic with the back of a wooden spoon or spatula to release its aroma. Do not let the garlic brown or it will become bitter.

Add the beans to the pan and stir to coat them with the oil. Stir in the tomatoes, chile, and ½ teaspoon salt. Raise the heat to medium and bring to a simmer, then reduce the heat to low and simmer gently until the beans are tender but not mushy and the sauce has thickened, 25–30 minutes. Remove from the heat and remove and discard the garlic. Stir in the basil. Serve right away.

WINE SUGGESTION: A MEDIUM-BODIED RED, SUCH AS CHIANTI CLASSICO

I love the lacinato kale used ubiquitously in Italian cooking, but I am also fond of the more readily available curly kind. Both types have an appealing, hearty texture and a sweet note. Kale is also nourishing and highly flavorful, especially when enhanced with a little crispy pancetta.

sautéed kale with pancetta & onion

3 oz (90 g) pancetta, finely chopped

1 tablespoon extra-virgin olive oil

½ small red onion, cut into ¼-inch (6-mm) dice

8 oz (250 g) baby kale leaves

Fine sea salt and freshly ground black pepper

1 tablespoon balsamic vinegar

serves 4

In a large, dry frying pan over medium heat, sauté the pancetta until lightly crisped and a little of the fat is rendered, about 7 minutes. Using a slotted spoon, transfer to paper towels to drain.

Add the olive oil to the pan and stir in the onion. Sauté until the onion is softened, about 6 minutes. Add the kale and, using tongs, turn to coat the greens with the fat in the pan. Season with salt and pepper and sprinkle in the vinegar. Cook, tossing occasionally, until the greens are just tender, 7–8 minutes. They should still be a bit crunchy but no longer taste raw.

Pile the kale in a serving bowl or on a serving platter and sprinkle the pancetta on top. Serve hot or warm.

WINE SUGGESTION: CHIANTI CLASSICO OR OTHER SANGIOVESE-BASED RED FROM TUSCANY

As soon as fall is upon us, I turn to these sturdy, assertively flavored greens, a favorite of my family. This is a versatile side dish for sausages, roast chicken, or pork chops, or you can toss it with cooked pasta or scrambled eggs.

white wine–braised broccoli rabe with olives

1¼ lb (625 g) rapini (broccoli rabe), tough stems removed

2 large cloves garlic, minced

3 tablespoons extra-virgin olive oil

½ cup (2½ oz/75 g) pitted cured black olives, coarsely chopped

2 imported Italian or Spanish anchovy fillets, finely chopped

1 small fresh hot chile, seeded and minced, or a generous pinch of red pepper flakes

1 cup (8 fl oz/250 ml) dry white wine

Fine sea salt

serves 4

Bring a large saucepan of water to a boil over high heat. Add the rapini and cook just until wilted, 3–4 minutes. Drain and let cool for 5 minutes, then chop very coarsely.

In a large frying pan over medium-low heat, warm the garlic in the olive oil, stirring often, until the garlic is softened but not browned, about 7 minutes. Stir in the olives, anchovies, and chile and sauté until fragrant, about 1 minute.

Raise the heat to medium and add the rapini to the pan, stirring to combine the greens with the olives and anchovies. Pour in the wine, raise the heat to medium-high, and bring to a simmer. Reduce the heat to medium-low, cover partially, and braise until the rapini is tender and most of the liquid has been absorbed, 15–20 minutes. Season with salt, if needed, and serve right away.

WINE SUGGESTION: A RICH WHITE, SUCH AS FALANGHINA OR FIANO DI AVELLINO

Red endive looks like a happy union between Belgian endive and radicchio. I use it often because it reminds me of all the varieties of radicchio grown in Italy's Veneto region. When baked, endive loses its bitter edge and turns mellow.

baked red endive with tomatoes & pancetta

2 tablespoons extra-virgin olive oil, plus more for greasing

4 heads red Belgian endive, cut in half lengthwise (use white if you can't find red)

1 carrot, peeled and finely chopped

1 rib celery, finely chopped

2 oz (60 g) pancetta, minced

1 clove garlic, minced

Fine sea salt and freshly ground black pepper

¼ cup (2 fl oz/60 ml) dry white wine

1 cup (7 oz/220 g) canned diced tomatoes

½ cup (2 oz/60 g) freshly grated Parmigiano-Reggiano cheese

serves 4

Preheat the oven to 350°F (175°C). Lightly oil an 8-inch (20-cm) square baking dish.

In a large frying pan, heat the olive oil over medium heat. Arrange the endive halves in the dish, cut side down. Cook, turning once, until browned on both sides, about 4 minutes per side. Using a slotted spatula, transfer the endive halves to the prepared dish, cut side up.

Add the carrot, celery, pancetta, and garlic to the frying pan and sauté over medium heat until the vegetables have begun to soften, about 5 minutes. Add ½ teaspoon salt and pepper to taste and sauté until the vegetables are soft and the pancetta is starting to crisp, about 5 minutes. Raise the heat to medium-high and pour in the wine. Cook until most of the wine has evaporated, about 1 minute. Stir in the tomatoes and bring to a simmer. Reduce the heat to medium-low and cook until the sauce has thickened, about 10 minutes.

Spoon the sauce over the endive halves, cover with aluminum foil, and bake for 1 hour. Uncover and sprinkle with the cheese, then bake, uncovered, until the top is golden brown, about 20 minutes longer. Let cool for 5 minutes, then serve.

WINE SUGGESTION: A WHITE FROM FRIULI, SUCH AS THOSE FROM THE DISTRICTS COLLIO OR COLLI ORIENTALI DEL FRIULI

One chilly spring in Garfagnana, in the alps of Tuscany, we warmed up with this *sformato*—a molded casserole that lies somewhere between a custard and a soufflé—of baked mashed green beans.

baked green bean custard

1 lb (500 g) green beans, stem ends removed

2 tablespoons unsalted butter, plus more for greasing

½ yellow onion, finely chopped

Fine sea salt and freshly ground black pepper

¾ cup (3 oz/90 g) freshly grated Parmigiano-Reggiano cheese, plus 2 tablespoons

2 tablespoons heavy cream

Pinch of freshly grated nutmeg

1 large egg, lightly beaten

3 tablespoons dried bread crumbs

1 tablespoon extra-virgin olive oil

serves 4

Preheat the oven to 375°F (190°C).

Place a steamer basket in a large saucepan and fill the pan with water up to but not touching the bottom of the basket. Bring the water to a boil over high heat. Add the beans to the basket, cover, and steam until very tender, 7–8 minutes. Remove from the heat and remove the basket from the pan.

In a large frying pan over medium-low heat, melt the butter. Add the onion and sauté until soft and translucent, 7–8 minutes. Add the green beans and ½ teaspoon salt. Mash the beans and onion to a coarse purée. Transfer to a bowl and add the ¾ cup (3 oz/90 g) cheese, the cream, nutmeg, and pepper to taste. Add the egg and fold the mixture together gently but thoroughly.

Lightly butter a small terrine or baking dish and sprinkle the bottom and sides with 2 tablespoons of the bread crumbs. Spoon the bean mixture into the dish and smooth the top.

In a small bowl, stir together the remaining 1 tablespoon bread crumbs, the olive oil, and the 2 tablespoons cheese and sprinkle over the *sformato*. Bake until the top is golden brown, 20–25 minutes. Serve hot or warm.

WINE SUGGESTION: A CRISP, LEMONY WHITE, SUCH AS GAVI DI GAVI OR VERNACCIA DI SAN GIMIGNANO

When I was growing up, potato pizza *al taglio* (by the slice) was my favorite snack while wandering through Rome. It had no sauce—just paper-thin slices of potatoes and a sprinkling of cheese and herbs. Here is my crustless twist on a Roman classic.

roasted potato & mushroom strata

3 tablespoons extra-virgin olive oil, plus more for greasing

1 lb (500 g) yellow waxy-skinned potatoes, such as Yukon gold, scrubbed but skins left on, very thinly sliced

8 oz (250 g) mixed fresh mushrooms, such as portobello, cremini, and shiitake, brushed clean and thinly sliced

2 cloves garlic, very thinly sliced

4 oz (125 g) shredded *Crucolo* or Asiago *fresco* cheese

1 tablespoon minced fresh flat-leaf parsley

2 teaspoons minced fresh oregano

Fine sea salt and freshly ground black pepper

serves 6–8

Preheat the oven to 425°F (220°C). Lightly oil a 12-inch (30-cm) round pizza pan or 9-by-13-inch (23-by-33-cm) baking dish.

Arrange one-third of the potato slices, slightly overlapping in a single layer, in the prepared pan. Scatter half of the mushrooms over the potatoes, followed by half of the garlic, half of the cheese, and half of the herbs. Drizzle 1 tablespoon of the olive oil over everything and sprinkle with a little salt and pepper. Repeat to make a second layer of potatoes, mushrooms, garlic, cheese, and herbs. Drizzle again with 1 tablespoon olive oil and season with salt and pepper to taste. Finish with a final layer of potatoes. Sprinkle with a little more salt and pepper and drizzle the remaining 1 tablespoon olive oil over the top.

Bake, uncovered, until bubbly and the potatoes are golden brown on top and crisped in spots, about 45 minutes. Let cool for 5 minutes, then cut into wedges and serve.

WINE SUGGESTION: GRECO DI TUFO, A RICH AND FRUITY WHITE FROM CAMPANIA

Fresh artichokes, both green and purple, start to appear in the Italian markets in March; they are arranged in beautiful piles and look like giant bouquets of flowers. Choose artichokes that feel heavy for their size and have tightly layered leaves.

sautéed artichokes & fava beans

Juice of 2 lemons

4 large artichokes

2 tablespoons extra-virgin olive oil

4 oz (125 g) pancetta, cut into ¼-inch (6-mm) dice

2 cloves garlic, very thinly sliced

½ cup (4 fl oz/125 ml) dry white wine

Fine sea salt and freshly ground black pepper

1 cup (5 oz/155 g) shelled, blanched, and peeled fava beans

2 tablespoons finely chopped fresh flat-leaf parsley

serves 4

Fill a bowl with cold water and add the lemon juice. Cut the stems off the artichokes, trim the end and tough skin around the stem, and place in the lemon water. Cut off the top one-third from the artichokes and remove the tough outer leaves. Cut the artichokes in half lengthwise and scoop out the fuzzy chokes with a spoon. Cut them in half again and immerse the quarters in the lemon water.

In a heavy-bottomed sauté pan, heat the olive oil and pancetta over medium heat. Sauté until the pancetta is lightly crisped, about 10 minutes. Add the garlic, reduce the heat to medium-low, and sauté until the garlic is softened, about 5 minutes. Drain the artichokes, reserving ½ cup (4 fl oz/125 ml) of the lemon water. Add the artichokes to the pan along with the reserved water, the wine, ½ teaspoon salt, and a little pepper. Raise the heat to medium-high and bring to a boil. Return the heat to medium-low, cover, and cook until the artichokes are almost tender but still a little firm, 15–20 minutes.

Stir in the fava beans. Cover and cook until the fava beans are tender, about 10 minutes. Uncover, raise the heat to medium, and cook until most of the liquid has been absorbed, about 5 minutes longer. Remove from the heat and stir in the parsley. Transfer to a serving bowl, pour the pan juices over the top, and serve.

WINE SUGGESTION: FALANGHINA OR GRECO DI TUFO FROM CAMPANIA

desserts

I've developed a small obsession in recent years—honey! Wherever I travel, I purchase a jar of local honey. It's much better than what's available in the supermarket. For this cake, I like to use an assertive honey, such as wildflower or chestnut.

honey-mascarpone cheesecake with sour cherries

1½ cups (6 oz/185 g) almond biscotti crumbs

6 tablespoons (3 oz/90 g) unsalted butter, melted

1 tablespoon sugar, plus 1½ cups (12 oz/375 g)

Fine sea salt

1 lb (500 g) cream cheese, at room temperature

1¼ cups (15 oz/185 g) wildflower or other full-flavored honey, such as star thistle or tupelo

4 large eggs

½ teaspoon almond extract

Finely grated zest of 1 lemon, plus 2 tablespoons fresh lemon juice

1 lb (500 g) mascarpone

1 cup (8 oz/250 g) full-fat sour cream or Greek-style yogurt

5 cups (1¼ lb/625 g) pitted sour cherries

serves 12

Preheat the oven to 350°F (180°C). In a bowl, combine the biscotti crumbs, 5 tablespoons (3 fl oz/80 ml) of the melted butter, the 1 tablespoon sugar, and a pinch of salt. Use the remaining 1 tablespoon melted butter to grease the inside of a 9-inch (23-cm) springform pan with 3-inch (7.5-cm) sides. Press the crumb mixture evenly into the bottom and up the sides of the pan.

In a bowl, using an electric mixer set on high speed, beat the cream cheese briefly to soften. Pour in the honey and beat until well combined. Add the eggs, one at a time, beating after each addition and scraping down the sides of the bowl from time to time. Beat in the almond extract and lemon zest and juice. Finally, beat in the mascarpone and sour cream.

Pour the batter into the prepared pan and smooth the top. Bake for 45 minutes. Turn off the heat and leave the cake in the oven for 1 hour without opening the door. Transfer the cake to a wire rack and let cool to room temperature (the center will still jiggle a bit). Refrigerate the cake in the pan for at least 6 hours, preferably overnight.

Meanwhile, in a saucepan over medium heat, combine the cherries and the 1½ cups (12 oz/375 g) sugar. Bring the mixture to a simmer, stirring to dissolve the sugar. Cook until the cherries are tender and have darkened in color but are still whole, 10–15 minutes. Drain into a heatproof bowl through a fine-mesh sieve. Return the liquid to the saucepan (reserve the bowl) and continue to simmer until thickened to a syrup and reduced by about half, about 5 minutes longer. Put the cherries in the reserved heatproof bowl and pour the syrup over them. Let stand until ready to serve.

To unmold, run a knife around the inside edge of the cake pan. Remove the ring from the pan and place the cake on a serving platter. Spoon a mound of cherries into the center of the cake. To serve, cut the cake into wedges, arrange on individual plates, and spoon additional cherries and syrup on top of each.

WINE SUGGESTION: BRACHETTO D'ACQUI, A SWEET, FIZZY RED FROM PIEDMONT

Traditional shortbread was one of the first things I learned to bake, using a recipe I clipped out of the newspaper when I was a girl. As is my habit, I decided at one point that I needed to "Italianize" the recipe, and these savory wedges were born.

citrusy shortbread wedges with rosemary

1½ cups (7½ oz/235 g) unbleached all-purpose flour, plus more for dusting

½ cup (3 oz/90 g) rice flour

¾ cup (6 oz/185 g) sugar

1 teaspoon finely grated lemon zest, plus a few zest curls for garnish

1 teaspoon finely grated orange zest

½ teaspoon finely minced fresh rosemary

½ teaspoon flaky sea salt, such as fleur de sel

1 cup (8 oz/250 g) cold unsalted butter, cut into ½-inch (12-mm) dice, plus more at room temperature for greasing

makes 24 bars

Preheat the oven to 325°F (165°C).

In a food processor, combine the flours, sugar, grated lemon and orange zests, minced rosemary, and salt and pulse to mix. Scatter the butter cubes around the bowl and process just until the mixture is crumbly and a ball of dough begins to form. Turn the dough out onto a lightly floured work surface and gently pat it together.

Line an 8-inch (20-cm) round cake pan with a sheet of parchment paper long enough to overhang by a few inches on two sides. Lightly grease the parchment paper inside the dish with the room-temperature butter.

Press the shortbread dough into the prepared dish in an even layer. Bake until the edges are golden brown and the center is pale gold and set, 35–40 minutes. Transfer to a wire rack and let cool for about 10 minutes.

Using the overhanging parchment as handles, transfer the shortbread to a clean cutting board. Using a sharp knife, cut into wedges. Let cool completely, then arrange on a platter and serve.

WINE SUGGESTION: VIN SANTO, A CLASSIC TUSCAN DESSERT WINE

Citrus and chocolate is a classic pairing in Italian desserts. Here, the juice and zest of one lemon brightens the rich flavors of the chocolate and the olive oil in the cake.

lemon-chocolate olive oil cake

4 oz (125 g) bittersweet chocolate, coarsely chopped

2 cups (10 oz/315 g) unbleached all-purpose flour

2 teaspoons baking powder

¼ teaspoon fine sea salt

1 cup (8 oz/250 g) granulated sugar

3 large eggs

½ teaspoon pure vanilla extract

¾ cup (6 oz/185 g) full-fat Greek-style yogurt

Finely grated zest of 1 lemon, plus 2 tablespoons fresh lemon juice

¾ cup (6 fl oz/180 ml) extra-virgin olive oil, plus more for greasing

Confectioners' sugar for dusting

makes one 9-by-5-inch (23-by-13-cm) loaf cake; serves 8

Preheat the oven to 350°F (180°C).

Put the chocolate in the top of a double boiler and set over (but not touching) barely simmering water. Heat, stirring, until the chocolate has melted. Remove from the heat and let cool slightly.

In a bowl, whisk together the flour, baking powder, and salt. Set aside. In a large bowl, using an electric mixer set on high speed, beat together the granulated sugar and eggs until pale in color. Beat in the vanilla. Add half of the flour mixture, beating until just incorporated. Beat in the yogurt and lemon juice, and then the remaining flour mixture. With the motor running, beat in the olive oil just until smooth.

Scoop about one-third of the batter into a clean bowl and gently fold in the chocolate. Stir the lemon zest into the rest of the batter.

Lightly oil a 9-by-5-inch (23-by-13-cm) loaf pan. Fill the pan with alternating spoonfuls of the lemon and chocolate batters. Swirl a large, thin-bladed knife in an S pattern through the batters to create the marbled effect. Bake until a cake tester inserted into the center comes out clean, 45–50 minutes. Transfer to a wire rack and let cool for 20 minutes. Carefully invert the cake onto the rack, then place upright on a cutting board. Cut the cake into thick slices and arrange, slightly overlapping, on a platter. Dust with the confectioners' sugar and serve.

WINE SUGGESTION: FRANCIACORTA, A RICH AND CREAMY SPARKLING WINE MADE IN THE STYLE OF CHAMPAGNE

Nut tortes are popular throughout Italy. You'll find versions made with almonds, hazelnuts, pistachios, or walnuts, as in this recipe. I've added a cocoa powder dusting and an orange-scented caramel sauce for an elegant touch. Use the sauce sparingly; you just need a spoonful to enhance the cake.

walnut-espresso torte with burnt orange caramel

FOR THE CAKE

4 tablespoons (2 oz/60 g) unsalted butter, melted and slightly cooled

2½ cups (10 oz/315 g) walnut halves

4 large eggs, separated, at room temperature

1 cup (8 oz/245 g) granulated sugar

1 heaping tablespoon instant espresso powder

Fine sea salt

FOR THE BURNT ORANGE CARAMEL

1 cup (8 oz/245 g) granulated sugar

½ cup (4 fl oz/125 ml) fresh orange juice, strained, at room temperature

Cocoa powder for dusting

Confectioners' sugar for dusting

makes one 9-inch (23-cm) cake; serves 10–12

To make the cake, preheat the oven to 325°F (165°C). Generously coat a 9-inch (23-cm) springform pan with 1 tablespoon of the melted butter. Line the bottom with parchment paper and butter the parchment. Reserve the remaining butter. Using a nut grinder, a rotary cheese grater with small holes, or the small holes of a box grater, finely grind or grate the walnuts. (Don't use a food processor or the nuts will be too heavy.) Gently scoop into a bowl. Set aside.

In the bowl of a stand mixer fitted with the whisk attachment, combine the egg yolks, ¾ cup (6 oz/185 g) of the granulated sugar, and the espresso powder. Beat on high speed until thickened and pale. Drizzle in the remaining butter and beat until combined.

In a clean stand mixer bowl fitted with a clean whisk attachment, combine the egg whites and a pinch of salt. Beat on low speed until foamy. Raise the speed to high and beat until peaks begin to form. Gradually add the remaining ¼ cup (2 oz/60 g) granulated sugar and beat until the whites hold stiff, glossy peaks.

Scoop about one-third of the whites into the bowl with the yolk mixture. Sprinkle one-third of the walnuts over the top and gently fold together. Fold in another one-third of the whites and walnuts, then fold in the rest until no white streaks remain. Scrape the batter into the prepared pan.

Bake until the top is nicely browned and a cake tester inserted into the center comes out clean, about 45 minutes. Transfer the pan to a wire rack and let cool for 20 minutes. Run a knife around the inside edge of the pan. Remove the ring from the pan and let the cake cool to room temperature.

To make the burnt orange caramel, place the granulated sugar in a heavy-bottomed saucepan and shake it gently to distribute the sugar. Place over medium heat and cook, swirling the pan every so often as the sugar begins to melt and turn brown, about 10 minutes; some spots will cook and caramelize sooner than others. When all of the sugar is melted, remove from the heat and carefully pour in the orange juice; the caramel will spatter and clump up. Return the pan to medium heat and cook, stirring gently, until the clumps have dissolved and the caramel is deep brown, about 10 minutes. Let cool for 5 minutes, then pour into a bowl and let cool completely.

To serve, carefully invert the cooled cake onto a plate and gently remove the metal bottom. Peel off the parchment. Invert the cake onto a serving platter. Dust with cocoa powder and confectioners' sugar and serve with the caramel.

WINE SUGGESTION: A SWEET (DOLCE) MARSALA (SUPERIORE OR SUPERIORE RISERVA, NOT FINE, WHICH IS GENERALLY USED IN COOKING)

My son and I discovered this *crostata* one afternoon at Al Baralla, a small, traditional *osteria* in Lucca, with brick vaulted ceilings and impeccable service. I couldn't stop thinking about it, so I called them after we got home, and the proprietor kindly sent me the recipe.

ricotta & bittersweet chocolate crostata

2½ cups (12½ oz/390 g) unbleached all-purpose flour, plus more for dusting

½ cup (4 oz/125 g) granulated sugar

Finely grated zest of 1 small lemon

1 teaspoon baking powder

⅛ teaspoon fine sea salt

½ cup (4 oz/125 g) cold unsalted butter, cut into ½-inch (12-mm) dice

2 large eggs

1 lb (500 g) fresh sheep's milk ricotta or well-drained whole cow's milk ricotta

¼ cup (1 oz/30 g) confectioners' sugar

½ teaspoon pure vanilla extract

1 cup (8 fl oz/250 ml) heavy cream, plus 2 tablespoons

8 oz (250 g) best-quality bittersweet chocolate, coarsely chopped

2 tablespoons unsweetened cocoa powder

serves 8

In a food processor, combine the flour, granulated sugar, lemon zest, baking powder, and salt and pulse to mix. Add the butter and pulse until the mixture is crumbly. Add the eggs and process just until the dough begins to come together.

Turn the dough out onto a lightly floured work surface and knead it briefly. Divide the dough in half and pat into 2 disks. Wrap one half in plastic wrap and freeze for another use. Roll out the remaining disk into a 12-inch (30-cm) round. Carefully transfer the dough to a 10-inch (25-cm) round tart pan, gently pressing it into the bottom and up the sides of the pan. Trim the overhanging dough flush with the top of the pan sides. Refrigerate for at least 1 hour and up to overnight.

Preheat the oven to 350°F (180°C). Remove the tart shell from the refrigerator. Using a fork, prick the bottom of the crust in a few places. Bake until the edges are just beginning to turn golden, about 10 minutes. Transfer to a wire rack and let cool. Leave the oven on.

In a large bowl, combine the ricotta, confectioners' sugar, vanilla, and 2 tablespoons heavy cream and stir to mix. Spoon the mixture into the crust. Bake until the filling is set, 20–25 minutes. Transfer to the wire rack and let cool to room temperature.

In a heatproof bowl, combine the chocolate and cocoa powder. In a small saucepan over medium heat, heat the 1 cup (8 fl oz/250 ml) cream until bubbles form around the edges. Pour the hot cream over the chocolate and stir until the mixture is glossy, dark, and smooth. Carefully spread the chocolate topping over the cooled filling, starting in the middle and creating a thick layer that stops just short of the crust.

Refrigerate the crostata until thoroughly chilled, about 2 hours. Remove the sides from the pan and place the crostata on a serving platter. Let stand for 30 minutes, then cut into wedges and serve.

WINE SUGGESTION: VIN SANTO, A CLASSIC TUSCAN DESSERT WINE

A homey cake is a treat any time of year. This simple rendition celebrates September, when farmers' markets are overflowing with small, dark Italian plums. Halved and nestled in the batter, the plums turn ruby red and jammy as they bake.

plum-almond cake

½ cup (4 fl oz/125 ml) sunflower or vegetable oil, plus more for greasing

1 cup (5 oz/155 g) unbleached all-purpose flour, plus more for dusting

½ cup (2 oz/60 g) almond meal or almond flour

2 teaspoons baking powder

¼ teaspoon fine sea salt

1 large egg

½ cup (4 fl oz/125 ml) half-and-half or whole milk

Finely grated zest and juice of 1 large lemon

1 cup (8 oz/250 g) sugar, plus 2 tablespoons

¼ teaspoon pure almond extract

9 Italian plums, halved and pitted

¼ cup (1 oz/30 g) sliced almonds

2 tablespoons unsalted butter, at room temperature

makes one 8-inch (20-cm) cake; serves 8

Preheat the oven to 375°F (190°C). Lightly oil an 8-inch (20-cm) springform pan. Dust the pan with flour and tap out the excess.

In a large bowl, whisk together the flour, almond meal, baking powder, and salt. In a separate bowl, combine the oil, egg, half-and-half, lemon zest and juice, the 1 cup (8 oz/250 g) sugar, and almond extract. Whisk to blend thoroughly. Add the wet ingredients to the flour mixture and whisk until just combined.

Pour the batter into the prepared pan. Arrange the plum halves, cut side up, on top of the batter. In a bowl, combine the almonds, the 2 tablespoons sugar, and the butter and mix well. Dot the almond topping over the cake.

Bake until the topping is golden brown and a cake tester inserted into the center of the cake comes out clean, about 45 minutes. Transfer to a wire rack and let cool for 20 minutes. Remove the ring from the pan and place the cake on a serving platter. Cut into wedges and serve warm or at room temperature.

WINE SUGGESTION: A SWEET MALVASIA, SUCH AS MALVASIA DI CASORZO DOLCE

When I was a girl, my family arrived in Italy each summer just as apricots were coming into season. I've eaten bushels of the fruit over the years, and still cherish their distinctive flavor. Blackberries add a touch of sweetness to this beautiful tart.

free-form blackberry-apricot tart

FOR THE CRUST

2 cups (10 oz/315 g) unbleached all-purpose flour, plus more for dusting

½ teaspoon granulated sugar

¼ teaspoon fine sea salt

¾ cup (6 oz/185 g) cold unsalted butter, cut into ½-inch (12-mm) dice

⅓ cup (3 fl oz/80 ml) ice water

1 lb (500 g) fresh apricots, pitted and quartered

1 cup (4 oz/125 g) blackberries

2 tablespoons unbleached all-purpose flour

⅓ cup (2½ oz/75 g) firmly packed light brown sugar

Pinch of freshly grated nutmeg

1 teaspoon unsalted butter, cut into small pieces

1 tablespoon half-and-half or whole milk

serves 6

To make the crust, in a food processor, combine the flour, granulated sugar, and salt and pulse to mix. Scatter the butter cubes around the bowl and process just until the mixture resembles coarse crumbs. With the motor running, drizzle in the ice water and process just until a ball of dough begins to form. Turn the dough out onto a lightly floured work surface and pat it into a disk. Wrap tightly in plastic wrap and refrigerate for at least 1 hour and up to overnight. Remove the dough from the refrigerator about 20 minutes before you plan to roll it out.

Preheat the oven to 375°F (190°C). In a large bowl, combine the apricots and blackberries. In a small bowl, stir together the flour, brown sugar, and nutmeg and sprinkle over the fruit. Fold in gently.

On a lightly floured work surface, roll the dough out into a 15-inch (38-cm) round. Carefully transfer the dough round to a large baking sheet. Pile the fruit mixture in the center, leaving a border of about 2 inches (5 cm) free of fruit. Dot with the butter. Fold up the edges of the dough to create a pleated border, partially covering the fruit. Brush the crust with the half-and-half.

Bake the *crostata* until the crust is golden brown and the exposed fruit is browned in spots, 30–35 minutes. Cut into wedges and serve warm.

WINE SUGGESTION: VIN SANTO, A CLASSIC TUSCAN DESSERT WINE

Add a splash of Marsala wine to buttery classic American pound cake and the flavor becomes distinctly, uniquely Italian—all the better when lightly lacquered with a wine-spiked syrup and garnished with a spoonful of glistening fruit compote.

marsala pound cake with dried fruit compote

1½ cups (12 oz/375 g) unsalted butter, at room temperature, plus more for greasing

3 cups (15 oz/470 g) unbleached all-purpose flour, plus more for dusting

1 teaspoon fine sea salt

3¼ cups (26 oz/815 g) sugar

6 large eggs

1 teaspoon pure vanilla extract

1 cup (8 fl oz/250 ml) dry Marsala wine

1 cup (8 oz/250 g) mascarpone or sour cream

1 small strip lemon zest

Preheat the oven to 325°F (165°C). Lightly butter a 10-inch (25-cm) tube pan. Dust the pan with flour and tap out the excess.

In a bowl, whisk together the flour and the salt. Set aside. Put the 1½ cups (12 oz/375 g) butter in a large bowl and, using an electric mixer set on medium speed, beat briefly to soften. Raise the speed to high and add 3 cups (24 oz/750 g) of the sugar, ½ cup (4 oz/125 g) at a time. Beat until the mixture is pale and fluffy, about 5 minutes. Add the eggs, one at a time, beating after each addition and scraping down the sides of the bowl from time to time. Beat in the vanilla.

Reduce the speed to medium and add about one-third of the flour mixture, beating until incorporated. Beat in ⅓ cup (3 fl oz/80 ml) of the wine, followed by another one-third of the flour mixture. Finally, beat in the mascarpone and the rest of the flour mixture until fully incorporated.

Scrape the batter into the prepared pan and smooth the top. Bake until the top is nicely browned and a cake tester inserted into the center comes out clean, about 1 hour 15 minutes.

FOR THE COMPOTE

3 cups (1 lb/500 g) dried fruit, such as figs, apricots, prunes, and cherries or cranberries

1 cinnamon stick

4 whole cloves

½ teaspoon pure vanilla extract

¾ cup (9 oz/280 g) honey

¾ cup (6 fl oz/180 ml) dry Marsala wine

Spiced Ricotta Ice Cream (page 199) or vanilla ice cream for serving (optional)

serves 12–16

Meanwhile, in a small saucepan over medium heat, combine the remaining ¼ cup (2 oz/65 g) sugar, the remaining ⅔ cup (5 fl oz/170 ml) wine, and the lemon zest and bring to a boil. Simmer gently until the mixture has thickened to a syrup, about 10 minutes. Remove from the heat, discard the lemon zest, and cover to keep warm.

While the cake is baking, make the compote: In a saucepan over medium-high heat, combine the dried fruit, cinnamon stick, cloves, vanilla, and honey. Pour the wine over the fruit and add 1¼ cups (10 fl oz/310 ml) water. Bring to a boil. Reduce the heat to medium-low and simmer gently until the fruit is soft and the sauce has thickened to a syrup, 15–20 minutes. Let cool slightly before serving.

When the cake is done, transfer to a wire rack and let cool for 20 minutes. Invert the cake onto a serving plate and remove the pan. While the cake is still warm, brush the top and sides with the warm Marsala syrup. Let cool to room temperature. Cut into wedges and serve with the warm compote and a scoop of the ice cream, if you like.

WINE SUGGESTION: PASSITO DI PANTELLERIA, FROM THE ISLAND OFF SICILY

Not far from my aunts' house in Rome was a *pasticceria* filled with sweet treasures. My favorite was a truly decadent confection—two large meringue cookies sandwiched together with whipped cream and drizzled with chocolate. I've pared it down for this restrained but delicious adaptation.

chocolate-dipped hazelnut meringues

4 large egg whites, at room temperature

½ teaspoon cream of tartar

½ teaspoon fine sea salt

1 cup (7 oz/220 g) superfine sugar

1 teaspoon pure vanilla extract

1¼ cups (6 oz/185 g) hazelnuts, toasted, skinned, and coarsely chopped (see Cook's Note, page 62)

5 oz (155 g) bittersweet chocolate, coarsely chopped

1 tablespoon vegetable oil

makes about 40 cookies

Position 2 racks in the lower third of the oven and preheat to 275°F (135°C). Line 2 large baking sheets with parchment paper.

In the bowl of a stand mixer fitted with the whisk attachment, combine the egg whites and cream of tartar. Beat on medium speed until foamy. Sprinkle in the salt. Raise the speed to high and beat in the sugar, 1 tablespoon at a time. Beat in the vanilla. At this point, the egg whites should hold stiff, glossy peaks that curl at the tips. Using a silicone spatula, gently fold in the hazelnuts.

Drop rounded teaspoonfuls of the meringue onto the prepared baking sheets. (If you want more uniformly shaped meringues, spoon the meringue into a pastry bag and pipe it onto the parchment-lined pans.)

Place the baking sheets in the oven and bake until the edges of the meringues are pale golden, 35–40 minutes. Turn off the heat and leave the meringues in the oven for 30 minutes without opening the oven door. Remove the baking sheets from the oven. Using a spatula, gently transfer the meringues to wire racks to cool completely. Reserve the parchment-lined baking sheets; you will use them after you dip the meringues in chocolate.

Put the chocolate in the top of a double boiler and set over (but not touching) barely simmering water. Heat, stirring, until the chocolate has melted. Stir in the oil. Remove from the heat.

Carefully pick up a meringue and dip the bottom into the hot chocolate, letting the excess drip off. Set the meringue, chocolate side down, on a reserved parchment-lined baking sheet. Dip the remaining meringues into the chocolate in the same way. Place in the freezer until the chocolate sets, about 5 minutes. Store the meringues in airtight containers, using a sheet of parchment paper to separate the layers, at room temperature for up to 1 week.

WINE SUGGESTION: A SWEET (DOLCE) MARSALA SUPERIORE OR SUPERIORE RISERVA

The first time I had *panna cotta*, at a restaurant in Rome near the Spanish Steps, it was served in a balloon glass, and the custard was rich and thick and tasted of pure cream and vanilla. This springtime version is served with a tart, bright rhubarb compote.

vanilla bean panna cotta with roasted rhubarb

FOR THE *PANNA COTTA*

4 cups (32 fl oz/1 l) heavy cream

⅔ cup (5 oz/155 g) sugar

½ vanilla bean

1 envelope (¼ oz/7 g) unflavored gelatin

FOR THE RHUBARB COMPOTE

1 lb (500 g) rhubarb, trimmed and thinly sliced (4 to 5 cups)

1 cup (8 oz/250 g) sugar

½ vanilla bean

serves 8

To make the *panna cotta,* in a large saucepan, combine the cream and sugar. Scrape the seeds from the vanilla bean into the cream mixture and add the pod. Cook over medium heat until the sugar has dissolved and the mixture is almost at a simmer, about 7 minutes. Remove from the heat, cover, and let steep for 20 minutes.

Pour 3 tablespoons water into a small bowl. Sprinkle the gelatin over the water and let stand for 5 minutes.

Uncover the cream and bring just to a simmer over medium heat. Gently whisk in the gelatin mixture, then remove from the heat. Discard the vanilla bean pod. Pour the panna cotta into 8 dessert cups or into a decorative bowl. Cover with plastic wrap and refrigerate until completely set, at least 3 hours and up to overnight.

Meanwhile, make the rhubarb compote: Preheat the oven to 375°F (190°C). In a baking dish, combine the rhubarb, sugar, and vanilla bean half. Cover with aluminum foil and bake until the rhubarb is very tender, about 45 minutes. Let cool slightly. Discard the vanilla bean.

Unmold the panna cotta onto small dessert plates, spoon a little of the rhubarb compote onto each serving, and serve.

WINE SUGGESTION: BRACHETTO D'ACQUI, A SWEET, FIZZY RED FROM PIEDMONT

For this luscious frozen dessert—*semifreddo* is Italian for "half cold"—be sure to wait for strawberry season, when you can find perfectly ripe, exquisitely perfumed fruit bursting with flavor.

frozen strawberry-yogurt mousse

2 pints (1 lb/500 g) strawberries, hulled

½ cup (4 oz/125 g) granulated sugar

2 tablespoons fresh lemon juice

2 cups (1 lb/500 g) full-fat Greek-style yogurt

1½ cups (12 fl oz/375 ml) heavy cream

⅓ cup (1⅓ oz/40 g) confectioners' sugar

Canola oil for greasing

serves 10

Set aside 5 of the prettiest strawberries. In a blender or food processor, combine the remaining strawberries, the granulated sugar, and the lemon juice and process to a smooth purée. Transfer the purée to a large bowl, whisk in the yogurt, and set aside.

In another bowl, combine the cream and confectioners' sugar. Using an electric mixer set on high speed, beat until stiff peaks form. Gently fold the sweetened whipped cream into the strawberry-yogurt mixture.

Lightly oil a 6-cup (48–fl oz/1.5-l) metal ring mold. Gently spoon the strawberry mixture into the mold and smooth the top. Cover with plastic wrap and freeze until completely solid, at least 6 hours or up to overnight.

To serve, remove the *semifreddo* from the freezer and let stand for about 5 minutes. Remove the plastic wrap and place a platter upside down over the mold. Carefully invert the *semifreddo* onto the platter. (If necessary, briefly dip the bottom of the mold in hot water to loosen it before unmolding.)

Cut the reserved strawberries in half lengthwise and arrange them on top of the *semifreddo*. Cut into wedges and serve.

WINE SUGGESTION: PASSITO DI PANTELLERIA, FROM THE ISLAND SOUTHWEST OF SICILY

My sister, Maria, lives close to a creamery in the New Jersey hills, where they make dozens of artisanal cheeses, including a rich, sweet sheep's milk ricotta—the perfect base for this creamy gelato.

spiced ricotta ice cream with macerated berries

FOR THE ICE CREAM

1½ cups (12 fl oz/375 ml) whole milk

1½ cups (12 fl oz/375 ml) heavy cream

½ teaspoon ground cinnamon

¼ teaspoon freshly grated nutmeg

5 large egg yolks

1 cup (8 oz/250 g) sugar

12 oz (375 g) fresh sheep's milk ricotta or well-drained whole cow's milk ricotta

2 cups (8 oz/250 g) blueberries

1 cup (4 oz/125 g) raspberries

1 cup (4 oz/125 g) blackberries

½ cup (2 oz/60 g) sugar

2 tablespoons Grand Marnier or orange-flavored brandy

makes about 1 qt (1 l); serves 6

To make the ice cream, in a saucepan over medium heat, combine the milk, cream, cinnamon, and nutmeg and warm until the mixture just comes to a simmer. Remove from the heat.

In a bowl, whisk the egg yolks with the sugar until thick and pale yellow. Slowly drizzle in a ladleful of the hot milk mixture, whisking constantly to prevent the eggs from curdling. Whisk in another ladleful of the hot milk mixture, then slowly whisk the egg mixture back into the saucepan. Place over medium heat and cook, stirring constantly with a wooden spoon, until a custard forms that lightly coats the back of the spoon, about 15 minutes.

Strain the custard through a fine-mesh sieve into a heatproof bowl and let cool slightly. In a separate bowl, mash the ricotta with a fork until smooth, then whisk into the cooled custard. Place a sheet of plastic wrap directly on the surface of the custard to prevent a skin from forming. Refrigerate for at least 4 hours and up to overnight. Freeze in an ice-cream machine according to the manufacturer's instructions. Spoon the gelato into a container with a tight-fitting lid, cover, and freeze until hard, at least 2 hours.

Put the berries in a bowl and mash lightly with a fork. Stir in the sugar and the liqueur. Let stand at room temperature for 1 hour.

Divide the gelato among dessert bowls, spoon the fruit on top, and serve.

WINE SUGGESTION: A SWEET MALVASIA, SUCH AS THE MALVASIA DI CASORZO DOLCE

Unlike the artificial green stuff you often find, this pistachio ice cream is the real deal: a pale yellow cream rich with the toasted nuts for which Sicily is famous. The added chocolate makes it irresistible.

pistachio ice cream with shaved chocolate

¾ cup (4 oz/125 g) unsalted roasted pistachio nuts

6 tablespoons (3 fl oz/90 ml) whole milk, plus 1½ cups (12 fl oz/375 ml)

1½ cups (12 fl oz/375 ml) heavy cream

4 large egg yolks

1 cup (8 oz/250 g) sugar

Pinch of fine sea salt

⅛ teaspoon almond extract (optional)

3 oz (90 g) bittersweet chocolate, shaved or finely chopped

makes about 1 qt (1 l); serves 6

Put the pistachios in a food processor and pulse until coarsely chopped. With the motor running, drizzle in the 6 tablespoons (3 fl oz/90 ml) milk and process until a creamy paste forms, about 1 minute. Scrape the pistachio paste into a bowl.

In a saucepan over medium heat, combine the 1½ cups (12 fl oz/375 ml) milk and the cream and warm until just at the point of simmering. Remove from the heat.

In a bowl, whisk together the egg yolks, sugar, and salt until thick and pale yellow. Slowly drizzle in a ladleful of the hot milk mixture, whisking constantly to prevent the eggs from curdling. Whisk in another ladleful of the hot milk mixture, then slowly whisk the egg mixture back into the saucepan. Place over medium-low heat and cook, stirring constantly with a wooden spoon, until a custard forms that lightly coats the back of the spoon, about 15 minutes.

Strain the hot custard through a fine-mesh sieve into a heatproof bowl and let cool slightly, then whisk in the pistachio paste. Stir in the almond extract, if using. Place a sheet of plastic wrap directly on the surface of the custard to prevent a skin from forming. Refrigerate for at least 4 hours and up to overnight. Freeze the custard in an ice-cream machine according to the manufacturer's instructions. When the custard has thickened in the machine, add the chocolate and continue to mix just until well blended. Spoon the gelato into a container with a tight-fitting lid, cover, and freeze until firm, about 4 hours. Divide among dessert bowls to serve.

WINE SUGGESTION: A SWEET MOSCATO D'ASTI

One of my favorite melon varieties to use in this recipe is Canary, which sports a bright yellow rind. Its cream-colored flesh turns beautifully translucent when frozen into this refreshing granita.

melon ice with mint & basil

⅓ cup (3 oz/90 g) sugar

3 cups (1 lb/500 g) Canary, Crenshaw, honeydew, or other melon chunks (½–1 melon, depending on size)

½ cup (6 fl oz/180 ml) honey

2 tablespoons fresh lemon juice

1 teaspoon minced fresh basil, plus a few small leaves for garnish

1 teaspoon minced fresh mint, plus a few small leaves for garnish

serves 6

In a small saucepan over medium heat, combine the sugar and ⅓ cup (3 fl oz/80 ml) water and cook, stirring, until the sugar is completely dissolved, about 5 minutes. Let the syrup cool to room temperature, then refrigerate until thoroughly chilled, 3–4 hours or overnight.

Put a 9-by-13-inch (23-by-33-cm) metal baking pan in the freezer until well chilled, at least 1 hour.

In a food processor, combine the melon, honey, lemon juice, minced basil and mint, and the cooled syrup and process until smooth. Pour the melon mixture into the chilled pan and place, uncovered, in the freezer. Freeze for 30 minutes. Using a fork, scrape the ice crystals away from the sides of the pan and stir the mixture thoroughly. Continue to freeze, scraping every 30 minutes or so, until the granita is completely frozen into fluffy shards, about 1½ hours total. Spoon the granita into a container with a tight-fitting lid, cover, and freeze until serving time.

Divide the granita among 6 glass bowls, garnish with 2 or 3 herb leaves, and serve.

WINE SUGGESTION: A SWEET MOSCATO D'ASTI

My friend Marta owns a B & B in Sulmona, Italy, where she serves a simple but delicious chocolate cake spiked with red wine, which adds an underlying fruity note. I had a hunch that the same treatment would be just as good in a classic chocolate *budino*—and it is. This pudding is rich, so I usually serve it in espresso cups.

red wine–chocolate budino with cinnamon whipped cream

FOR THE *BUDINO*

2 cups (16 fl oz/500 ml) whole milk

1 vanilla bean, split

4 tablespoons (2 oz/60 g) unsalted butter

½ cup (4 oz/125 g) granulated sugar

Fine sea salt

⅓ cup plus 1 tablespoon (2 oz/60 g) unbleached all-purpose flour

½ cup (4 fl oz/125 ml) dry red wine, such as Montepulciano d'Abruzzo or Chianti

3½ oz (105 g) bittersweet chocolate, chopped

½ teaspoon ground cinnamon

FOR THE CINNAMON WHIPPED CREAM

¾ cup (6 fl oz/180 ml) heavy cream

1 tablespoon confectioners' sugar

⅛ teaspoon ground cinnamon

makes 6–8 regular servings or 12 mini servings

To make the *budino*, pour 1½ cups (12 fl oz/375 ml) of the milk into a saucepan. Scrape the seeds from the vanilla bean into the pan and add the pod. Place over medium heat and bring to a boil, stirring to break up the clumps of vanilla seeds. Remove from the heat, cover, and let steep for 10 minutes.

In a heavy-bottomed saucepan, melt the butter over medium-low heat. Stir in the granulated sugar and a pinch of salt and whisk to combine. Whisk in the flour; the mixture will thicken immediately. Reduce the heat to low, add the remaining ½ cup (4 fl oz/125 ml) milk and the wine, and whisk until smooth, about 1 minute. Add the chocolate and cinnamon, and whisk until the chocolate is melted and smooth.

Strain the vanilla-infused milk through a fine-mesh sieve into the chocolate mixture and cook, whisking continuously, until very thick, about 2 minutes. Pour the *budino* into a 4-cup (32–fl oz/1-l) mold or into individual ramekins, cappuccino or espresso cups, or wineglasses. Cover with plastic wrap and refrigerate until thoroughly chilled, at least 2 hours or up to overnight.

Just before serving, make the cinnamon whipped cream: In a chilled metal bowl, combine the cream, confectioners' sugar, and cinnamon and whip with an electric mixer until soft peaks form. Serve each pudding with a dollop of whipped cream.

WINE SUGGESTION: BRACHETTO D'ACQUI, A SWEET AND FIZZY RED FROM PIEDMONT

Good fresh figs are hard to come by, so that's why I recently planted my own fig tree in our backyard. I dream of the abundant harvests it will have one day. I suggest purchasing these sweet, delicate fruits whenever you see them—they're definitely worth the splurge.

baked figs with balsamic honey & black pepper

2 tablespoons wildflower or other full-flavored honey

1 tablespoon unsalted butter

1 tablespoon aged balsamic vinegar

½ teaspoon peppercorns, lightly crushed

Fine sea salt

Vegetable oil for greasing

12 ripe fresh Mission or Calimyrna figs

Small fresh mint sprigs for garnish

Mascarpone or vanilla ice cream for serving (optional)

serves 4–6

Preheat the oven to 425°F (220°C).

In a small saucepan, combine the honey, butter, vinegar, peppercorns, and a tiny pinch of salt. Warm over medium-low heat until the butter has melted and the mixture loosens into a sauce, about 5 minutes.

Lightly oil a 10-inch (25-cm) cast-iron frying pan or baking dish. Using a small, sharp knife and starting at the blossom ends, cut each fig into quarters, stopping just short of cutting through the stem ends so the quarters are still attached. Carefully arrange the figs standing upright in the prepared pan and nudge the cut ends open like flower petals. Spoon the sauce over the figs.

Bake until the figs are softened and lightly caramelized, 10–15 minutes. Using a large spoon, carefully transfer the figs to a serving platter and garnish with the mint sprigs. Place a dollop of mascarpone or vanilla ice cream next to the figs, if you like, drizzle with the sauce from the baking dish, and serve warm.

WINE SUGGESTION: VIN SANTO, A CLASSIC TUSCAN DESSERT WINE

Grilling nectarines concentrates the fruits' sweetness and imparts an earthy, almost savory flavor that pairs perfectly with a salty hard cheese and spiced honey, as in this summery dessert recipe.

grilled nectarines with pecorino & honey

¼ cup (3 oz/90 g) wildflower or other full-flavored honey, such as star thistle, summer thistle, or mesquite

1 tablespoon salted butter

¼ teaspoon aniseed, crushed

4 ripe but firm nectarines, halved and pitted

Small wedges of *pecorino romano* cheese for serving

serves 4

Prepare a fire in a charcoal grill or preheat a gas grill to medium-high.

In a small saucepan over medium-low heat, warm the honey with the butter and aniseed, stirring to help dissolve the honey, until the butter has melted and the mixture is fragrant, about 5 minutes.

Brush the cut sides of the nectarines generously with the honey mixture. Arrange the nectarines on the grill grate, cut side down, and cook until nicely grill marked and beginning to caramelize, 3–4 minutes. Turn and grill on the second side until slightly softened, about 3 minutes longer.

Place 2 nectarine halves on each of 4 dessert plates. Place a small wedge or two of cheese next to the nectarines and drizzle a little of the remaining honey mixture over the top of the fruit and cheese. Serve right away.

WINE SUGGESTION: PECORINO, A FRUITY WHITE FROM ABRUZZO OR LE MARCHE

basic recipes

CROSTINI

1 slender baguette (*ficelle*), cut crosswise on the diagonal into slices about ½ inch (12 mm) thick

Extra-virgin olive oil for brushing

MAKES ABOUT 24 CROSTINI

Preheat the oven to 400°F (200°C). Arrange the baguette slices on a large rimmed baking sheet and brush the tops with olive oil. Bake until the edges are lightly browned and the tops are golden, 8–10 minutes.

PIZZA DOUGH

2¾ cups (14 oz/440 g) bread flour, plus more for dusting

¼ cup (1½ oz/45 g) semolina flour

2 teaspoons rapid-rise yeast

1½ teaspoons fine sea salt

1 cup (8 fl oz/250 ml) warm water (100–110°F/38–43°C)

3 tablespoons extra-virgin olive oil, plus more for greasing

MAKES 1½ LB (680 G)

In a food processor, combine both flours, the yeast, and the salt and pulse briefly to mix. With the motor running, drizzle in the water and then the olive oil. Process just until a ball of dough forms.

Turn the dough out onto a lightly floured work surface and knead until smooth and elastic, 2–3 minutes. Pat back into a ball.

Lightly oil a large bowl. Put the ball of dough in the bowl and turn to coat with the oil. Cover the bowl with plastic wrap and let the dough rise in a warm spot until doubled in bulk, about 1½ hours.

Punch the dough down and knead briefly to remove any air bubbles. Roll out as directed in the recipe. If not using immediately, shape into a disk, transfer to a lock-top plastic bag, and refrigerate for up to 1 day or freeze for up to 1 month. Let the dough come to room temperature before using.

BASIC EGG PASTA DOUGH

2 cups (10 oz/315 g) unbleached all-purpose flour, plus more as needed

1 tablespoon semolina flour

½ teaspoon fine sea salt

Pinch of freshly grated nutmeg

3 extra-large eggs, lightly beaten

1–2 tablespoons extra-virgin olive oil

MAKES 1 LB (500 G)

In a food processor, combine the flours, salt, and nutmeg and pulse briefly to mix. Add the eggs and process briefly. Drizzle in 1 tablespoon of the olive oil and process until the mixture forms curdlike crumbs. When you pinch the dough it should form a soft ball. If it is too wet or sticky, add more flour, 1 tablespoon at a time, and process briefly. If it is too dry, drizzle in the remaining 1 tablespoon oil.

Turn the dough out onto a lightly floured work surface and knead until smooth and firm but pliable. This will take several minutes. Wrap the dough tightly in plastic wrap and let sit at room temperature for 30 minutes.

To roll out the dough, cut it into 4 equal pieces. Cover 3 pieces with plastic wrap. Briefly knead the fourth piece on a lightly floured surface. Set the rollers of a pasta machine to the widest setting, then crank the dough through the rollers. Fold the dough into thirds and pass it through the rollers again. Repeat folding and rolling two or three times until the dough is smooth. Reset the rollers one width narrower and crank the dough through the setting twice, then adjust the rollers to the next narrowest setting. Continue to pass the dough through the rollers twice on each setting until you have a long, very thin sheet.

Lay the dough sheet on a lightly floured surface and cut into 4-by-5-inch (10-by-13-cm) rectangles, or cut the sheet into noodles as directed in individual recipes. Repeat with the remaining 3 dough portions.

SPINACH PASTA DOUGH

9 oz (280 g) fresh spinach leaves
or 5 oz (155 g) thawed frozen
whole-leaf spinach

2 extra-large eggs

2 cups (10 oz/315 g) unbleached
all-purpose flour, plus more
as needed

2 tablespoons semolina flour

¾ teaspoon fine sea salt

Pinch of freshly grated nutmeg

Few drops of extra-virgin
olive oil, if needed

MAKES 1 LB (500 G)

In a saucepan over medium-high heat, combine the spinach and 2 tablespoons water, cover, and cook until the spinach is wilted and tender, 3–5 minutes. Drain into a colander in the sink. When cool enough to handle, squeeze with your hands to release as much moisture as possible.

In a food processor, combine the spinach and 1 of the eggs and process until puréed. Transfer to a small bowl. Wash and dry the processor bowl.

In the processor, combine both flours, the salt, and the nutmeg and pulse briefly to mix. Add the spinach purée and the remaining egg and process until the mixture forms curdlike crumbs. Pinch a little of the dough and roll it between your fingers. It should form a soft ball. If it is too wet or sticky, add more flour, 1 tablespoon at a time, and process briefly. If it is too dry, drizzle in the oil.

Follow the directions for Basic Egg Pasta Dough (left) to knead, roll out, and cut the dough.

BASIC TOMATO SAUCE

3 tablespoons extra-virgin olive oil

2 cloves garlic, lightly crushed
but left whole

1 can (28 oz/875 g) diced or
crushed tomatoes, with juice

1 can (15 oz/470 g) stewed tomatoes

Kosher or sea salt

10 fresh basil leaves, shredded or torn

MAKES 1½ QT (1.5 L)

In a large saucepan over medium heat, warm the olive oil. Add the garlic, heat until it begins to sizzle, and then press down on it with a wooden spoon to help release its flavor. Carefully stir in all of the tomatoes (the oil will spatter) and season with salt. Raise the heat to medium-high and bring to a boil. Reduce the heat to medium-low and simmer, uncovered, stirring occasionally, until thickened, about 30 minutes.

Remove from the heat and stir in the basil. Taste and adjust the seasoning. Use immediately, or let cool to room temperature, cover, and refrigerate for up to 3 days or freeze for up to 3 months.

CHICKEN BROTH

1 chicken, 4–5 lb (64–80 oz/1.8–2.2 kg)

2 whole cloves

2 yellow onions, quartered

3 carrots, cut into 2-inch (5-cm) pieces

2 ribs celery, including leafy tops,
cut into 2-inch (5-cm) pieces

1 cup (1½ oz/45 g) coarsely chopped
fresh flat-leaf parsley

4 fresh thyme sprigs (optional)

½ teaspoon peppercorns

Kosher or sea salt

MAKES 2–2½ QT (2–2.5 L)

Place the chicken in a large stockpot. Stick the cloves into 2 onion quarters and add them to the pot with the remaining onions, carrots, celery, parsley, thyme, and peppercorns. Add water to cover by about 2 inches (5 cm) and bring to a boil over medium-high heat, skimming any foam that forms on the surface. Reduce the heat to low and simmer gently, uncovered, skimming any foam as it appears, until reduced by about half, 3–4 hours. Season with salt during the last hour of cooking.

Lift out the chicken from the pot, remove the skin and bones, and reserve the meat for use in soups. Line a colander with damp cheesecloth and place over a clean container. Strain the broth through the colander. Let cool to room temperature, then cover and refrigerate until well chilled. Skim off and discard the congealed layer of fat on the surface before using. If not using immediately, refrigerate the broth for up to 3 days or freeze for up to 3 months.

wine guide

REDS

AGLIANICO An ancient grape believed to have been brought from Greece. Grown mainly in the Basilicata and Campania regions, it makes a robust and concentrated wine. Among the best is Aglianico del Vulture, grown near Mount Vulture, an extinct volcano.

BARBARESCO Along with Barolo, one of the great reds from Piedmont. Both wines are 100 percent Nebbiolo, though Barbaresco is generally modestly lighter and softer than the more celebrated (and expensive) Barolo.

BARBERA (D'ALBA OR D'ASTI) A grape that generally yields medium-bodied wines with crisp acidity that pair well with many foods. Barbera is grown widely in Italy, but the districts surrounding the towns of Alba and Asti in Piedmont turn out some of the finest examples.

BARDOLINO A light and snappy red from the area around Bardolino, a town on beautiful Lake Garda in northern Italy. A blend of the same grapes used in Valpolicella, the wine can also be found in a rosé (Bardolino Chiaretto) and a sparkler (spumante).

BAROLO Big, elegant wines made from the Nebbiolo grape that usually demand significant time in a cellar before they are ready to drink. Worth the splurge for a special occasion.

CANNONAU A bold red from the island of Sardinia. Cannonau is the Sardinian name for Grenache.

CERASUOLO An Italian rosé. Among the most interesting is Cerasuolo Montepulciano d'Abruzzo, which is cherry red and has an intense, nutty taste.

CHIANTI (CLASSICO, RISERVA) Perhaps the best-known Italian wine in America. Chianti is a Tuscan blend whose predominant grape is Sangiovese. The wines are generally medium bodied with a pleasantly bitter flavor, but styles vary widely. The Chianti region covers a vast swath of north-central Italy and includes eight subzones. The most famous, Chianti Classico, is at the center of the region, between Florence and Siena. Riserva on the label means the wine has been aged for at least three years.

DOLCETTO (D'ALBA OR DI DOGLIANI) An easy-drinking wine from Piedmont. Although dolcetto means "little sweet one," these wines are distinctly dry, sometimes with a slightly bitter, even smoky finish. Some of the best come from the districts of Alba and Dogliani.

LANGHE ROSSO A class of red made in the Langhe hills, near the Piedmontese town of Alba. The wines can vary significantly in style and quality. The surrounding area is home to some of Italy's best reds (including the three B's, Barolo, Barbaresco, and Barbera), and grapes used in those wines find their way into blends for Langhe Rosso.

MARSALA The famous fortified wine of Sicily, blended from several grapes native to the island. There are dry (secco), semisweet (semisecco), and sweet (dolce) styles, as well as different colors (Ambra and Oro are made with white grapes, Rubino with red). To pair with desserts, look for Marsala dolce; for an aperitif, try Marsala secco. There are several quality grades as well. For dolce styles, look for Superiore or Superiore Riserva on the label. For an aperitif, try Vergine, the highest grade of Marsala, made only in the dry style.

MONICA A grape believed to have been brought to Sardinia from Spain. Today, the grapes are used to make two Sardinian reds, Monica di Cagliari, which is 100 percent Monica, and Monica di Sardegna, a blend that includes other local grapes.

MONTEPULCIANO D'ABRUZZO A pleasant, everyday wine from Abruzzo. The plump, juicy grape grows easily in the region, where it is crushed into wines that are medium bodied and fruity.

MORELLINO DI SCANSANO An increasingly popular wine produced around Scansano, a village in the Maremma in southwest Tuscany. The Morellino grape is a strain of Sangiovese, and the wine is similar to Chianti and other Sangiovese-based wines of Tuscany.

NEGROAMARO The name of the grape means "black bitter," which says a lot about the wine it produces. Grown in Puglia since the sixth century BC, the grape makes rustic reds that are deeply colored and slightly bitter. It is also key to Salice Salentino, a blend of Negroamaro and Malvasia Nera.

NERO D'AVOLA A grape native to Sicily once used mainly as a blender with other varietals. Thanks to more careful viticulture and wine making, it has grown increasingly popular, offering rich, velvety, robust reds.

PINOT NERO The Italian version of Pinot Noir. Light and fruity, the wines are produced mainly in the north, with those from Alto Adige among the most successful.

PRIMITIVO Rustic and spicy wine made mainly in Puglia. The grape is genetically identical to Zinfandel.

SAGRANTINO DI MONTEFALCO A specialty of Umbria, blended from Sagrantino and Sangiovese grapes. These wines can be rich with hints of plum, prune, and dark cherries.

SALICE SALENTINO Named for a small town near the southern tip of Puglia. The wine is made by blending Negroamaro, the dark, bitter grape native to the province, with Malvasia Nera, which softens the wine's rough edges.

SANGIOVESE The grape that forms the backbone of Chianti and stars in the so-called super-Tuscans. Sangiovese grapes are also used in such classics as Vino Nobile di Montalcino and Brunello di Montalcino. As a solo varietal, Sangiovese can range from thin, everyday red to beautifully structured, robust wine.

SCHIAVA The red wines made from Schiava grapes are light-to-medium bodied with a refreshing acidity. Grown in Alto Adige, Schiava is also known by its German name, Vernatsch. The wines can be labeled with either name, or look for official wine classifications (DOCs) that are based on the grape, including St. Maddalena (St. Magdalener in German), Alto Adige DOC, and Lago di Caldaro (or Kalterersee). The wines can be a nice alternative to bigger Italian reds.

VALPOLICELLA (SUPERIORE, RIPASSO, AMARONE) Produced in an area near the northern city of Verona. The wine ranges from light to amazingly robust. Valpolicella is the easy-drinking, fruity red typically made from three local grapes, Corvina Veronese, Rondinella, and Molinara. The next step up is Valpolicella Superiore, aged for at least a year in wood and a bit sturdier as a result. Bigger yet is Valpolicella Ripasso, which is produced by allowing the wine to ferment for a second time on the grape skins left over from making Amarone. Finally, there is Amarone della Valpolicella, which wine writer Oz Clarke has called "a pretty strong beast." This robust red balances bitterness with intense, smoky fruit flavors of plum and cherries.

WHITES

ARNEIS (ROERO) An ancient grape grown in Piedmont that had virtually fallen out of production until it was revived in the 1960s. Alfredo Currado of Cantina Vietti led the way, conducting early wine-making experiments that set the stage for the renaissance. Roero Arneis is a medium-bodied white, crisp and well balanced.

CATARRATTO A Sicilian grape that produces a crisp, everyday white with notes of lemon. It is also used in Marsala and in blends such as Etna Bianco.

COLLI ORIENTALI DEL FRIULI One of the major wine districts of the northeastern region of Friuli, known for producing crisp, light white wines. Friulano is the main white grape of the region.

ETNA BIANCO A dry white with a minerally, flinty character made with grapes grown high on the slopes of Sicily's volcanic Mount Etna. Etna Bianco is at least 60 percent Carricante, with Catarratto and other local grapes making up the rest. Etna Bianco Superiore is at least 80 percent Carricante.

FALANGHINA A grape native to the southern region of Campania. It produces a rich, crisp wine, often with notes of pear, honey, and vanilla.

FIANO DI AVELLINO An elegant wine with delicate floral flavors that has been called "the thoroughbred" of the three lovely whites from Campania (Falanghina and Greco di Tufo are the other two).

FRIULANO A crisp white common in the Friuli region. It used to be known as Tocai Friulano, but that ended in 2007 by order of the European Union, which wanted to avoid confusion with Hungarian Tokaji. The Friulano grape is thought to be identical to the Sauvignon Vert grape grown in Chile.

GAVI An aromatic, flinty white made from the Cortese grape in northwest Italy. Only the wines made within the town of Gavi may carry the label Gavi di Gavi.

GRECO DI TUFO One of the oldest grapes grown near Avellino, in Campania, believed to be Greek in origin. The wine of the same name is crisp, with mineral and lemon notes.

GRILLO A Sicilian grape used in Marsala. The grape is now increasingly used in a crisp, everyday white of the same name.

INZOLIA A fresh and citrusy white from Sicily, made from the grape of the same name. Also used in Marsala.

MALVASIA A mainstay of Italian dessert wines. Grown throughout Italy, Malvasia shows up in a variety of styles, usually sweet and often carrying rich flavors of apricot and peach. In Sicily and Sardinia, it stars in *passito*-style wines, which are made with fruit that has been dried on straw mats.

NURAGUS An ancient grape of Sardinia, thought to have been brought to the island by the Phoenicians. Nuragus di Cagliari is a light, crisp everyday white.

ORVIETO The center of production for this white blend is the Umbrian town of the same name. Orvieto is a crisp, peachy white made from Trebbiano, Grechetto, and several other local grapes. Orvieto Superiorede notes higher quality, and Orvieto Classico means the wine comes from the original zone surrounding the town. Most Orvieto is dry, but there is also the Orvieto Amabile, which is on the sweeter side.

PASSITO DI PANTELLERIA A dessert wine made from the Moscato grape on the island of Pantelleria. The lovely sweet, golden wine has the scent of orange blossoms and a modest acidity.

PECORINO An heirloom grape native to Abruzzo and the Marche that yields a viscous, soft wine. Pecorino refers to sheep, and legend has it that the grape was so named because animals loved to venture through the vineyards eating the fruit. The grape had fallen out of widespread production until a rebirth in the 1990s.

PIGATO A grape variety (primarily known as Vermentino elsewhere) grown in the coastal region of Liguria. It produces refreshing, pleasantly tangy wines.

PINOT GRIGIO The seemingly ubiquitous white from northern Italy (made from a grape that originated in France). Much of the Pinot Grigio sold today is unremarkable or worse, so avoid the cheapest options. Wines from Alto Adige can be high quality.

SOAVE One of many Italian wines whose quality has been improving as a result of more careful viticulture and wine making. A venerable wine from the Veneto region, Soave still varies in quality. At its best, it is crisp, bracing, and intense. Look for Soave Superiore, which should be a step up.

TREBBIANO A white grape grown in many parts of Italy. It is used to make everyday wines and as a blender with other varietals.

VERDICCHIO (DEI CASTELLI JESI OR DI METALICA) A classic white from the Marche region. It is a substantial wine with good acidity and the flavors of nuts and lemons.

VERMENTINO (BOLGHERI, DI SARDEGNA, DI GALLURA) A grape that thrives on the island of Sardinia. Vermentino di Gallura is among the finest Vermentinos produced in Italy. The robust, acidic white is also found along the coast in Liguria and in Tuscany, where Vermentino Bolgheri is made.

VERNACCIA DI SAN GIMIGNANO The best-known wine to carry the name Vernaccia in Italy. This refreshing, acidic white with a pale straw color, is produced around the Tuscan town of San Gimignano.

VIN SANTO A traditional sweet Tuscan dessert wine. It is usually made with Trebbiano or Malvasia grapes that have been allowed to dry on straw mats to concentrate their sugar content. It is traditionally served after a meal with biscotti.

SPARKLING

BRACHETTO (D'ACQUI) A sweet, fun, and fizzy red from Piedmont.

FRANCIACORTA A sparkling wine from the northern region of Lombardy. Franciacorta is richer and more complex (and more expensive) than Italy's better-known sparkler, prosecco. It must be made using the same traditional method that produces Champagne, in which the bubbles are produced by a secondary fermentation that takes place in each bottle (the secondary fermentation for prosecco and many other sparkling wines happens in pressurized tanks). The grapes used in Franciacorta are similar to those in Champagne: Chardonnay, Pinot Bianco, and Pinot Nero. The result can be creamy and full-bodied.

MOSCATO (D'ASTI) A light, crisp semi-sparkler (frizzante style) made from grapes of the same name. The better-known Asti Spumante, made from the same grape, is a fully sparkling wine. Look to artisanal producers for the best versions.

PROSECCO Travelers to northern Italy's Veneto region know that restaurants routinely welcome guests with a glass of this sparkler. Prosecco, from the grape of the same name, is a dry, fruity, and casual bubbly. The grape is grown throughout the Veneto, but wines from two zones, prosecco di Conegliano and prosecco di Valdobbiadene, tend to be the best.

cheese & salumi guide

CHEESE

ASIAGO A cow's milk cheese from the Veneto region. In texture, it ranges from semifirm to hard, depending on how long it is aged. Semifirm (fresh) Asiago is moist and salty, ideal for melting; aged Asiago is crumbly and savory and makes a good grating cheese.

BURRATA A moist, fresh cheese made from buffalo's or cow's milk. Like mozzarella, *burrata* is a *pasta filata*—"stretched curd"—cheese. The stretched curd encloses a filling of mozzarella scraps and cream, which slowly flows out when you cut into the cheese.

CAMBOZOLA A soft-ripened cow's milk blue. Invented around 1900, it is a hybrid of French camembert and Italian Gorgonzola.

CRESCENZA A fresh cow's milk cheese from Lombardy traditionally made in autumn and winter, when the butterfat content of milk is at its highest. It has a thin, delicate rind and a moist, almost-runny paste. When kept in a warm place, the cheese rises through its thin rind; hence the name, from the Italian verb *crescere*, "to grow." It has a fresh, clean taste.

FONTINA A semifirm, washed-rind cow's milk cheese produced in Val d'Aosta, near the French and Swiss borders. The rind is reddish brown and the paste is dense and supple. Although the aroma is fairly intense, the flavor—slightly pungent and mushroomy—is less so.

GORGONZOLA A blue-streaked cow's milk cheese produced in large drums in parts of Lombardy and Piedmont. The reddish white rind is slightly sticky and the texture and flavor of the paste change as the cheese ages. The less aged Gorgonzola *dolce* is creamy and soft, salty with a sweet finish. Gorgonzola *piccante* is more crumbly and has a sharper flavor.

GRANA PADANO A hard cow's milk cheese created in the twelfth century by Cistercian monks in the Po Valley, in Lombardy. A classic grating cheese, *grana* ("grain" in Italian) is made from partially skimmed milk and has a craggy, crumbly texture and a buttery, savory flavor.

LA TUR A soft-ripened cheese produced in Piedmont made from a blend of three milks, cow, goat, and sheep. The delicate rind is gorgeously crinkled, and the interior is creamy and fluffy, with a fresh, rich, and acidic flavor.

MASCARPONE A fresh triple-cream cheese traditionally made from the milk of cows that have grazed on grass, flowers, and herbs. It has a dense, smooth spreadable texture and fresh, sweet taste. Mascarpone is typically used in desserts such as tiramisu, but can also be stirred into pasta or risotto.

MONTASIO A semifirm to hard cow's milk cheese produced in Friuli. The cheese is aged for at least sixty days and up to ten months. The interior is lightly pocked, with a texture that changes as the cheese ages from smooth to hard and granular.

MOZZARELLA A fresh *pasta filata* (stretched curd) cheese made from the milk of cows or water buffalo. Fresh mozzarella is milky and slightly tangy, with a springy texture. It is typically served fresh, especially with tomatoes in summer, or as a topping for pizza.

PARMIGIANO-REGGIANO An aged raw-milk cheese from Emilia-Romagna made from partially skimmed cow's milk. It has a rich, sharp, savory flavor and a hard, crumbly texture shot through with tiny protein crystals. Look for the words Parmigiano-Reggiano stamped on the hard brown rind, indicating that the cheese has been made according to strict rules.

PECORINO A general term referring to certain Italian cheeses made with sheep's milk that are mild when fresh and young, but become hard, salty, and sharp when aged. The most well-known is *pecorino romano*, which is produced in areas outside of Rome. *Pecorino sardo*, from Sardinia, and *pecorino toscano*, from Tuscany, are two other well-known variations.

PIAVE A hard cheese made from partially skimmed cow's milk in the Piave River Valley in the Veneto. A young *piave* has a smooth, dense texture. An aged *piave* is often compared to Parmigiano-Reggiano and, like its better-known peer, is an excellent grating cheese with a rich, nutty, slightly fruity flavor.

PROVOLONE A semifirm *pasta filata* (stretched curd) cow's milk cheese that was originally produced in southern Italy but is now also produced elsewhere. It is typically fashioned into the shape of a large sausage or a pear. The cheese has a thin, hard golden rind. Young provolone (aged two to three months) is smooth and mild. Aged provolone (*piccante*) is crumblier, with an assertive, spicy flavor.

RICOTTA A fresh, soft, mild cheese made from whey, a by-product of cheese making. Italian ricotta is made from the whey of sheep's, cow's, buffalo's, or goat's milk, though sheep's milk ricotta is most common.

RICOTTA SALATA A pressed, salted, and dried variation of ricotta cheese. It is chalky white and crumbly and can be sliced, crumbled, or shredded.

ROBIOLA A luxurious pillow of soft-ripened mixed-milk cheese (usually cow's, goat's, and sheep's milk) produced in Lombardy and Piedmont. The soft, bloomy rind is edible and the paste is creamy and luscious, with a salty, slightly tangy taste. Numerous variations exist.

SCAMORZA A *pasta filata* (stretched curd) cow's milk cheese that is similar to mozzarella, except that it is aged slightly to produce a firmer, drier cheese. The cheese is formed into a ball and a string is tied around the top so that it can be hung to dry. This results in the cheese's classic teardrop shape with a small top knot. *Scamorza affumicata* (smoked scamorza) is also common. It is a great shredding and melting cheese.

SOTTOCENERE AL TARTUFO A semisoft cow's milk cheese produced in the Veneto. The cheese is aged under ash (*sottocenere* means "under ash") that has been spiked with herbs and spices. The paste is studded with bits of black and white truffles, and the cheese is rubbed with truffle oil.

SOVRANO A hard, craggy grating cheese similar to Parmigiano-Reggiano, but made in Lombardy from a mix of cow's and buffalo's milk. It has an appealing salty taste and a slight tang that pairs well with antipasto flavors, such as briny olives and roasted peppers.

TALEGGIO A square-shaped washed-rind semisoft cheese made in Lombardy and Piedmont. It has a pungent aroma but is milder in flavor—tangy and appealingly meaty, with a fruity finish. It has a soft buttery texture that makes it perfect for spreading.

TOMA PIEMONTESE A cylindrical cheese made in Piedmont from either whole or partially skimmed cow's milk. The rind changes color from yellow to reddish brown as the cheese ages. The paste is ivory colored and smooth with small holes. The flavor ranges from sweet and mild to full and nutty as the cheese ages.

UBRIACO A firm, aged cow's milk cheese from Friuli that is bathed in wine and covered in pressed grape skins salvaged from wine making. It typically has a smooth white interior with a fruity flavor and a purple-brown rind.

SALUMI

BRESAOLA An air-dried lean beef originally produced in the Valtellina area of Lombardy. Cured with salt and spices, *bresaola* has little or no visible fat and is deep red to purple-red. It is typically sliced paper-thin and served as part of a platter of salumi or antipasti.

COPPA Heavily seasoned (either spicy or sweet) cured pork. The meat (typically pork shoulder) is cut into chunks and stuffed into casings and dried. It should be sliced paper thin for serving.

GUANCIALE Cured and dried pork jowl that is used to flavor dishes such as *bucatini all'amatriciana* and *spaghetti alla carbonara*. It has a more pronounced flavor than the more common pancetta.

MORTADELLA A large, smooth, pink forcemeat sausage studded with peppercorns, pistachios, and lardons and poached. The resulting sausage has a beautifully silky texture. It should be sliced thin for sandwiches or salumi platters, but it can be diced or cubed for recipes.

PANCETTA Pork belly—the same cut of meat used to make bacon—cured with salt and spices but not smoked. It is typically rolled and hung to dry for a couple of weeks, but can also be dried flat. It is used to flavor sauces and dishes and to top pizzas.

PROSCIUTTO Salt-cured and air-dried ham traditionally produced in the Parma area of Emilia-Romagna and San Daniele in Friuli-Venezia Giulia and aged for up two years according to strict standards. Also known as *prosciutto crudo*, the best prosciutto has a silky, buttery texture and a deep rose color streaked with white fat. It is served thinly sliced and goes beautifully with melon, figs, or fresh mozzarella.

SALAMI Dried cured sausages that vary widely from region to region. Differences depend on many factors, including the ratio of lean meat to fat, the type of meat mixture used, how coarsely the meat is ground, which spices are used, and whether the sausage is smoked during curing. Black pepper, crushed red pepper, garlic, and fennel are regularly used to flavor salami.

SPECK Cured and smoked ham produced in Alto Adige. The meat is cured with salt and spices, including juniper berries and bay leaf; smoked over beech, ash, or juniper wood; and then aged. It is served both thinly sliced and diced and is also used in cooking.

italian pantry staples

BEANS Italians often call beans the poor man's meat because they are so high in protein. Look for imported dried beans in Italian markets. Good-quality canned beans are a convenient alternative. Rinse well and drain before using.

Borlotti These popular, mild-flavored beans sport an attractive pink-beige background speckled with maroon. They typically appear in *pasta e fagioli* (pasta and beans), a classic peasant dish, and in minestrone. Similarly speckled cranberry beans are a good substitute.

Cannellini Ivory-colored beans of moderate size with a fluffy texture when cooked, cannellini are the signature beans of Tuscany. They are often served warm, drizzled with extra-virgin olive oil, either as a topping for bruschetta or used in *contorni*. White kidney beans or Great Northern beans can be used in their place.

Fava Pale green fava beans look like lima beans but have a slightly bitter flavor. Tuscans call them *baccelli* and serve the tender spring harvest raw with young pecorino cheese. Shelling favas requires two steps: slip the beans from their pods, and then blanch and remove their skins.

Romano Also called Italian beans, these edible-pod beans have broader, flatter pods and a more robust flavor and texture than the more common green beans.

CAPERS The preserved buds of a wild shrub, capers have a piquant flavor enjoyed throughout the Mediterranean. Capers packed in sea salt retain their intense floral flavor and firm texture best, but brined capers are more commonly available. Rinse both types before using.

FARRO Grown primarily in Tuscany and Umbria, *farro* has a deliciously nutty, wheatlike flavor and high protein content. It is used in soups and salads or cooked like risotto. Look for pearled *farro*, which is partly hulled and cooks more quickly than whole-grain *farro*.

FLOUR Italians classify their flour as 1, 0, or 00, which refers to how finely milled it is and how much of the husk and grain of the wheat have been removed. Since Italian flour is difficult to locate outside Italy, other, more readily available types can be used.

All-purpose Also known as plain flour, all-purpose flour is made from a mixture of soft and hard wheats. It can be used for making some pizza and pasta doughs.

Almond Also known as almond meal, almond flour is simply finely ground nuts. You can make it yourself by toasting the nuts and grinding them in a food processor. Be careful you do not grind too long, or you'll release the nut oils and end up with almond butter.

Cake Low in protein, high in starch, and finely textured, cake flour, also known as soft-wheat flour, is milled from soft wheat and is used primarily for delicately crumbed cakes. It is similar to the standard flour Italian cooks use for both savory and sweet recipes.

Rice Milled from either white or brown rice, this flour is used mainly for baked goods and desserts. Cake flour or pastry flour can be substituted.

Semolina This somewhat coarse flour is milled from high-protein durum wheat. It is typically used in the manufacture of dried pastas and is called for in some pizza and bread doughs.

LENTILS The Castelluccio plains in Umbria yield a native crop of lentils. These are petite, brownish green, and retain their shape when cooked. Look for them at specialty-foods stores or online retailers. French Puy lentils can be substituted.

OILS Flavor and smoke point are the two primary considerations when choosing an oil. Oils with a high smoke point are ideal for sautéing and frying. Highly flavorful oils, such as extra-virgin olive oil and toasted hazelnut oil, have a low smoke point and are best kept for drizzling on finished dishes.

Hazelnut oil Richly flavored hazelnut oil is pressed from untoasted or toasted nuts (the latter has a more distinctive taste). It is used as a condiment and salad dressing, sometimes cut with a milder oil to mellow the flavor. Buttery nut oils are perishable, so once opened, store in the refrigerator and use within a few months.

Olive oil Italy and other countries in the Mediterranean region produce excellent olive oils. Processing young olives yields green oils such as those from Tuscany (look for oil labeled *olio nuovo*). Mature olives, like those harvested in southern Italy, produce a golden, buttery oil. The highest grade is labeled "extra-virgin," which refers to cold pressing the fruit without the use of heat or chemicals. At their best, extra-virgin oils are clear, greenish, and taste fruity and sometimes slightly peppery. Save your best oils for finishing dishes.

OLIVES The bitter fruit of a hardy tree, olives must be cured before they can be eaten. Brine-cured olives stay plump, smooth, and relatively firm. Salt- or oil-cured olives become dry, wrinkled, and pleasantly bitter. Color depends on when the fruit was harvested.

Black, cured The dark, shriveled oil-cured olives produced mainly in Morocco are delicious, but they are strongly flavored and rather salty. Olives that seem too salty can be blanched for a minute, then drained.

Cerignola From southern Italy, large and meaty Cerignola olives are sold green, red, or black, or mixed together for a trio of colors.

Gaeta A brownish black, soft, and smooth salt-cured olive from Italy, with a nutty flavor.

Kalamata Purplish black, almond shaped, and meaty, this popular Greek olive is cured in brine and then packed in oil and vinegar.

Niçoise Small, brownish black olives from Provence. Brine cured and then packed in oil with lemon and herbs, they have a mellow, nutty flavor.

Picholine Green, smooth, and salty medium-sized olives from France.

Sicilian Large, green, tart, and meaty olives sometimes flavored with red pepper or fennel.

POLENTA The term refers to both uncooked cornmeal and the thick, porridgelike dish made from it. Soft polenta can be topped with a hearty sauce, accompany roast meat, or be swirled with cheese for a simple meal on its own. Cooled and cut into pieces, it can also be fried or grilled. Seek out a coarse-ground polenta imported from Italy.

RICE Three main varieties of rice are used in Italy to cook risotto. Best known is Arborio rice, preferred in the kitchens of Lombardy, Emilia-Romagna, and Piedmont. Its plump, oval grains are rich in the surface starch that produces the distinctive creamy character of risotto. The best Arborio is grown in the Po Valley. Vialone Nano rice, a favorite in the Veneto for its smaller grains, has less surface starch and yields firmer-textured, less creamy risotto. Carnaroli, the most costly variety of the three, is a specialty of the Novara and Vercelli areas of northern Italy and combines the creaminess of Arborio with the firm texture of Vialone Nano.

TOMATOES In the Italian kitchen, tomatoes are sliced and eaten raw, used to make sauce for pasta and pizza, and added to soups and stews.

San Marzano A variety of plum tomato grown in southern Italy, the San Marzano is widely acknowledged as the gold standard of sauce tomatoes (both fresh and canned) due to its meaty texture and deep flavor.

Sun-dried Drying tomatoes in the sun intensifies their flavor and yields a dense and chewy texture. Packed in oil, they are flavorful, pliable, and ready to add to cooked dishes. If dry packed, they are sometimes rehydrated in hot water before using.

VINEGARS The term *vinegar* refers to any alcoholic liquid caused to ferment a second time by certain strains of yeast, turning it highly acidic. Vinegars highlight the qualities of the liquid from which they are made. Red wine vinegar, for example, has a more robust flavor than vinegar produced from white wine. Both varieties are indispensable to the Italian pantry.

Balsamic vinegar *Aceto balsamico tradizionale* comes from Emilia-Romagna and is made from the cooked must of Trebbiano and Lambrusco grapes. The finest examples are aged for at least twelve years. Slightly thick and syrupy, with a sweet, mellow taste, it is used sparingly as a condiment. Less-expensive versions are widely available and can be used in vinaigrettes, marinades, and other preparations.

index

weldon**owen**

1045 Sansome Street, Suite 100, San Francisco, CA 94111
www.weldonowen.com

Weldon Owen is a division of

BONNIER

WELDON OWEN, INC.

President & Publisher Roger Shaw
SVP, Sales & Marketing Amy Kaneko
Finance Manager Philip Paulick

Associate Publisher Amy Marr
Associate Editor Emma Rudolph

Creative Director Kelly Booth
Art Director Marisa Kwek
Photo Director Alexandra Zeigler
Senior Production Designer Rachel Lopez Metzger

Production Director Chris Hemesath
Associate Production Director Michelle Duggan

Director of Enterprise Systems Shawn Macey
Imaging Manager Don Hill

Photographer Maren Caruso
Food Stylist Robyn Valarik
Prop Stylist Glenn Jenkins
Illustrator Margaret Berg

Rustic Italian

Conceived and produced by Weldon Owen, Inc.
In collaboration with Williams-Sonoma, Inc.
3250 Van Ness Avenue, San Francisco, CA 94109

A WELDON OWEN PRODUCTION
Copyright © 2015 Weldon Owen, Inc.
and Williams-Sonoma, Inc.
All rights reserved, including the right of
reproduction in whole or in part in any form.

Printed and bound in China by 1010 Printing, Ltd.

First printed in 2015
10 9 8 7 6 5 4 3 2

Library of Congress Cataloging-in-Publication
data is available.

ISBN 13: 978-1-61628-963-8
ISBN 10: 1-61628-963-5

ACKNOWLEDGMENTS

Weldon Owen wishes to thank the following people
for their generous support in producing this book: Kris Balloun, Gloria Geller,
Peggy Fallon, Penny Flood, Isabella Martinez, and Elizabeth Parson